After Rejection

God's Path to Emotional Healing

By Jonas Clark

Unless otherwise noted, Scripture quotations are taken from the King James Version.

LIFE After Rejection, God's Path to Emotional Healing
ISBN-10: 1-886885-22-2
ISBN-13: 978-1-886885-22-6

Copyright © 2007 by Jonas Clark

Published by Spirit of Life Publishing
27 West Hallandale Beach Blvd.
Hallandale, Florida
33009-5437, U.S.A.
(954) 456-4420

www.JonasClark.com

Library of Congress Control Number: 2002093363

01 02 03 04 05 06 07 ·· 07 06 05 04 03 02 01

ABOUT THE AUTHOR

Jonas Clark is a refreshing voice and a champion in the contemporary Church. Jonas served God for more than two decades as a pastor, teacher and evangelist before the Lord called him to his role as an apostle in the end time Church.

An evangelist at heart, Jonas travels around the world preaching the Gospel with a bold apostolic anointing. Fortitude and God's grace have taken his ministry into more than 25 countries, where he delivers a message of salvation, healing, deliverance and apostolic reformation. His passion is to win lost souls for Jesus Christ and equip every believer to take the Good News into the harvest fields to fulfill the Great Commission.

Jonas is the founder of The Global Cause Network, an international network of believers and Champion partners united to build a platform for the apostolic voice. He also heads Spirit of Life Ministries, a multi-cultural, non-denominational church in Hallandale Beach, Florida.

Jonas is the publisher of *The Voice* magazine, a print media platform that offers Prophetic Revelation for the Apostolic Revolution.

You can also watch him nationwide on the **Kingdom Living with Jonas Clark** television broadcast.

Dedicated to Nichole

"On the mount of great horses sit those with God's courage. Stand fast young champion, the greatest race is still ahead -- your life."

Love Dad

Once I looked for a cloud in the sky. The harder I looked the higher it seemed. Then one day I didn't look anymore. To my surprise it wasn't there.

What have you stopped looking for?

by Jonas Clark

CONTENTS

FOREWORD

I am seeing a new breed of ministers beginning to come forth in the apostolic move. Ministers who are completely sold out to the cause of Jesus Christ, men and women willing to lay down their lives to send the Gospel message around the world. These ministers deny themselves in order to see the Body of Christ set free and its members step into the fullness of their callings.

One of these modern apostles is Jonas Clark. Jonas has been ministering to the Body of Christ for 25 years, fulfilling his call as an apostle to the nations. From the day that I first met him, he has greatly influenced my life by challenging me, prompting me, and stretching me. With his encouragement, I have done things I would never have attempted on my own.

In my 28 years of ministry, I have found a common denominator in the lives of those who fight insecurity, inferiority, and depression. That common denominator is rejection. In *Life After Rejection*, Jonas exposes the tool of rejection the enemy uses against the Church. Jonas draws from his many years of experience in ministering to hurting people. His transparency in sharing his own battles with rejection reminds us that we all have pain and that Jesus has come to heal our broken hearts.

One of the most powerful aspects of this book is the way in which the Holy Spirit took Jonas behind the scenes in the lives of many of the great men and women in the Bible who experienced failure because they failed to recognize and deal with rejection in their lives. Rejection is one of the tools in Satan's arsenal that makes us unable to function in the Church. There are many wonderful, gifted and anointed members of the Body of Christ whose gifts and ministries have been neutralized by rejection. Let's learn from the mistakes of those mentioned in this book so that we don't fall into the same traps and miss our rewards.

I am convinced that after reading this book, each reader will be able to locate the root of the pain in their lives so they can receive the healing provided for in the atonement of Jesus Christ. It is often said, "Hurting people hurt people." If the Church is to stop hurting one another, the pain must first be stopped in each of us. The pain we hold causes walls to be built between our family, friends, our God, and us. This book is definitely a key to the healing that the Body of Christ must experience in order to work together in taking the Gospel of Christ to the world.

Jonas has written this book under the unction of the Holy Spirit. As you read it, let that anointing minister to you and destroy the yokes of bondage that have kept you from fulfilling your call.

Thank you, Jonas, for being a vessel that God can use to bring healing to His Body.

David Coker
Gateway Christian Fellowship
Carnesville, Georgia

PREFACE

The pain of rejection is one of the most horrible hurts we face in our lives. Rejection's torment is almost unbearable, and impossible to describe.

When I was a little boy, my parents argued and abused each other continually. One day my only sister drowned in the canal behind our house. She was four years old. Even though I was only six years old at the time, I distinctly remember my mother's desperate cries for help to the 9-1-1 dispatcher. I also remember the paramedic's frantic efforts to revive my sister – without success. The spirit of grief seemed to permeate our home. From that day forward the climate in our home grew worse. My mother blamed my father, who in turn blamed my mother for the death of my beautiful sister.

Somehow I felt that I, too, was to blame. The pain of that tragic day was too much for them to bear, and my parents separated when I was only nine years old. When my father left, I felt abandoned. I could only wonder why he left us. I immediately internalized the pain and took the burden of blame on my little shoulders. I also wondered what I had done wrong. That day the pain of rejection entered my heart and it affected me for many years. Like many of you I discovered that rejection is hell. But I also discovered that therethere is life after rejection. The Holy Spirit can heal every wound, no matter how long it's been there.

As you read the following pages, my prayer is that you will be able to understand the root of rejection, and how to achieve freedom from its intolerable assignment. I pray you will experience the same healing, freedom and love of Jesus that I did. He will give you peace that will not go away. You can experience life after rejection.

Your partner,

Jonas Clark

Chapter 1

THE HOUSE
REJECTION BUILT

Rejection is among the most prevalent hindrances to spiritual maturity in the Body of Christ. That's because deep-seated rejection leads to personality malfunctions that stunt a person's emotional growth. It grieves me to see how many people are conditioned to respond to life through hurts, wounds, pains, and scars from the past. We could sum it up this way: Rejection builds houses with defective construction materials that eventually crumble.

We can better understand why people who are struggling with rejection feel and act the way they do by taking the time to dissect the various elements of rejection. We can also gain godly insight into this personality malfunction by studying the ways God's people dealt with rejection throughout the Scriptures. By exploring the roots of rejection and examining how biblical characters dealt with overwhelming emotions we can learn to receive God's healing, renew our minds, respond and behave differently, and finally, become all that God wants us to be. We can escape the pain of rejection once and for all. Yes, there is life after rejection and it belongs to you.

Over the years I've met thousands of people just like you who suffered at the hand of rejection. It is astounding to realize just how this mental malady impacts the lives of so many people. We've all experienced rejection to some degree. For some, it's a mild discomfort. For others, it's a living hell. But before we can break free from rejection, we need to understand what we are dealing with. What exactly is rejection?

Rejection is the feeling of not being liked, loved, valued, or received. It is the state of feeling unwanted, unaccepted, or unappreciated.

Notice the common thread in the definition: feelings. People with rejection-based personalities internalize their feelings. Over the years, this internalization creates a false personality. This false personality is what I refer to as 'the house rejection built.' The following emotions are associated with rejection:

- Worthlessness.

- Wishing you had never been born.

- Inferiority.

- Guilt.

- Shame.

PERSONALITY MALFUNCTION

People living under the cloud of rejection measure their self-worth based on whether other people accept them. When others don't accept them – or when they don't "feel" accepted – they reject themselves. This has an obvious and negative impact on their personality.

Rejection creates a personality malfunction based on hurts and wounds in the wake of circumstances such as:

- Feeling left out.

- Generational curses.

- Divorce.

- Betrayal.

- Emotional trauma.

- Abandonment.

- Neglect.

- Abuse of any kind.

REJECTION'S CONSTRUCTION MATERIALS

Whether the circumstances that cause a person to adopt a rejection complex is real or imaginary is irrelevant to people suffering from this emotional handicap. The root cause of a rejection-based personality malfunction is purely and simply pain. Satan takes advantage of our pain and uses it to convince us to erect a house (personality) with rejection's building materials

Typically, a person with a rejection-based personality has spent years building a house made of ungodly bricks and mortar. Rejection's construction materials build a personality that tends to:

- Have a gloomy outlook on life.

- Fear people's opinion of them.

- Always trying to fit in but never really feeling they belong.

- Think good things belong to everyone but them.

- Seek the attention and approval of others.

Through prayer and deliverance we can bring about healing, but the false personality rejection built must be torn down brick by brick. Only then can our personalities be rebuilt through renewing the mind with the Word of God and resisting the devil's lies about who we are.

We must learn how to separate emotions from truth. The Word of God will divide between soul and spirit. Rejection wants to tell you who you are – and it's not the confident person God created you to be. Rejection wants you to get your value and self-esteem through works rather than through Christ in you. People suffering from rejection lean on works to establish self-worth. These people may eventually wear themselves out being people-pleasures or become introverted and do nothing at all. After all, they figure, what's the use? It's never enough. Alternatively, rejection-based personalities may become overbearingly extroverted and use work to prove themselves to others at all costs. We must learn to identify the stimuli that trigger feelings of rejection, understand the sources of this over sensitivity, and submit them to the truth of God's Word.

APERÇU

Rejection is a feeling of not being liked, accepted, loved, valued, or received.

People with rejection-based personalities internalize their feelings of rejection, which create, over the years, a false personality.

The root cause of a rejection personality malfunction is pain.

Rejection creates a personality disorder caused by hurts, wounds, pain, generational curses, divorce, trauma, abandonment, neglect, or abuse.

Through prayer and deliverance we can bring about healing, but the false personality rejection built must be torn down bit by bit. Only then can our personalities be rebuilt through renewing the mind with the Word of God and resisting the devil's lies about who we are.

Rejection wants to tell you who you are, give you value and self-esteem through works rather than an identity provided by Christ.

Chapter 2

THIS OLD HOUSE

Rejection wants to give you a skewed identity. It is a force that will try to mold your personality into something pitiful. If you are suffering from rejection, remember this: the rejected personality is not the real you. The real you is hidden under the mask of rejection. The good news is you can take off that mask and live the life God has purposed for you. There is life after rejection. It's a life of love, acceptance, joy and peace.

We can't let our hurts of yesterday decide our identity today. You are who God says you are. Renewing your mind with the Word of God is the first step toward freedom from rejection. If we do not think right, then we cannot believe right. If we do not believe right, then we will never be able to act right. It is important to understand that we cannot trust our soulish nature to tell us who we are. The house that rejection built is supplied with inner agony and an endless struggle to feel accepted. Past experiences, however, will always taint and falsely color the way we see ourselves and the way we respond to those around us. In other words, even when we are accepted we may not feel accepted.

> The rejected personality is not the real you.

RENOVATING THE OLD HOUSE

Again, our rejected experiences have built a house according to the designs of pain and hurt. If we want to get free from the past we will eventually have to undertake one of two projects, depending on how much damage has been done. Sometimes we need to renovate our minds with the truth of God's Word. But, like any renovation, sometimes the damage is so deep or so old that renovation turns into complete reconstruction. In those cases, the old house must be torn down to its foundation and built again.

Remember, freedom from rejection depends, in part, on the success of your renovation project. So what does renew mean and how do we undertake this renovation project? Let's look to God's Word for answers.

> "And be not conformed to this world: but be ye transformed by the renewing (renovation) of your mind, that ye may prove what is that good, and acceptable, and perfect, will of God" (Romans 12:2).

The English Word transformed stems from the Greek Word *metamorphoo*, meaning to be changed into another form. This suggests the Word of God, when used to renovate our minds, will gradually morph us into the proper personality. It promises life after rejection by the washing of the water of the Word. Notice Romans 12:2 deals with the mind of man and not the spirit of man. When you repented of your sins and asked Jesus for forgiveness, you became a new creature in Christ Jesus,

> "Old things are passed away; behold, all things are become new" (2 Corinthians 5:17).

That dealt with your spirit man, however, the real you. But your soul man still had issues that needed to be dealt with. The soul of man is the mind, will, intellect, reasoning, imaginations and emotions. All of these must be conformed to the will of God through submission to the Word of God. Only then can our personalities be morphed into our proper, Christ-like identities. Don't look at the Word of God's ability to renovate our minds through the eyes of unbelief. Meditating on God's Word will bring freedom from even the deepest pain if we only believe. But if we reject the knowledge of God, the pain of rejection will continue to tell us who we are. Rejection is a liar. God's word is truth. Applied knowledge of the Word of God is key to the success of our renovation project. We don't need to understand how or why it works. We need only have faith and be doers of the word to find life after rejection.

Remember the words the Lord spoke through the Prophet Hosea:

"My people are destroyed for lack of knowledge: because thou hast rejected knowledge, I will also reject thee...." (Hosea 4:6)

REJECTING KNOWLEDGE

Rejection of knowledge (God's Word) gives rejection the right to continue to operate. The Word teaches us that if we are "hearers only" and not "doers of the Word" of God, then we "deceive ourselves." Doubtless, if we deceive ourselves we will continue to walk in the rejected personality. The applied Word of God is our key to victory!

> "But be ye doers of the Word, and not hearers only, *deceiving your own selves*. For if any be a hearer of the Word, and not a doer, he is like unto a man beholding his natural face in a glass: For he beholdeth himself, and goeth his way, and straightway forgetteth what manner (sort) of man he was. But whoso looketh into the perfect law of liberty, and continueth therein, he being not a forgetful hearer, but a doer of the work, this man shall be blessed in his deed." (James 1:22-25, italics added)

The English word in the Bible that reads deceive stems from the Greek Word *paralogizomai*, meaning to:

- Reckon wrongly.

- Cheat yourself.

- Have a false reasoning.

- Delude.

- Avoid.

> Renovation is a process of tearing down the learned behavior that rejection built.

The bottom line is this: Deception is a condition that is caused by refusing to walk out (obey) the Word of God. Yes, there may have and probably was an event that sent rejection knocking at your door. But you have to let it into your house. This is tough love, but I have to be honest with you. It is impossible to renovate your mind with truth if you do not obey the truth. Renovation is a process of tearing down the learned behavior that rejection built. The truth we obey is the truth that will tear down the rejected personality.

In the next chapter, we will begin to examine the causes of rejection.

APERÇU

The rejected personality is not the real you.

Rejection wants to give you a false identity.

The house that rejection builds is furnished with inner agony and an endless struggle to feel accepted.

Past experiences will always taint and falsely color the way we see ourselves and respond to those around us.

Renewing our minds with the Word of God is the first step toward freedom with those who suffer from rejection.

Freedom from rejection depends, in part, on the success of your renovation project.

The English Word transformed stems from the Greek Word *metamorphoo*, meaning to be changed into another form.

The soul of man is the mind, will, intellect, reasoning, imaginations and emotions. All of these must conform to the will of God through submission to the Word of God.

Applied knowledge of the Word of God is key to our renovation project.

The truth we obey is the truth that will tear down the rejected personality.

Chapter 3

TRAITS OF REJECTION

Everyone comes face-to-face with rejection. It is a part of everyday life. We can't avoid rejection because we can't control the way people feel about us. Some will like us automatically; others may reject us without reason. The good news is, however, we can control our response.

What does rejection in everyday life look like? Well, people might be turned down for pay raises, refused job promotions, declined for loans, taken for granted

> We can't avoid rejection because we can't control the way people feel about us.

by peers, treated poorly by family, and passed over for due recognition. All of these are real life situations in which people are rejected. It may not seem as dramatic as a divorce or an abuse, but it's rejection all the same. So why do some face more difficulty handling every day rejections than others? Could it have more to do with the feelings that are set off inside their souls even at the slightest hint of rejection? Consider this: Is rejection an emotional response or an objective response to life? Does rejection push a button causing some sort of internal process that calculates a lessened self-worth? As we continue along in our study, let's explore the possibility the negative feelings rejection causes are rooted in the improper internalization of external events.

CAUSES OF REJECTION

Each of us has the basic need to feel accepted. Rejection is the feeling (internalization) that we are not being valued or accepted. When we do not feel accepted, then we must learn how to deal with the negative feelings of that rejection because we cannot depend on being accepted by others to give us our sense of self-worth. Jesus Christ makes us worthy, and we are "accepted in the beloved" (Ephesians 1:6).

Before we can properly respond to rejection events, we must pinpoint the source of the feelings. This is what I call rejection's trigger. Rejection's trigger must be dismantled. Interestingly, there are almost as many causes for rejection as there are people. Causes of rejection can stem from:

- A lack of love from a spouse, parent, or grandparent.

- An unwanted pregnancy.

- The trauma of divorce.

- The abandonment by a friend or loved one.

- A violation of trust.

- Abuse, whether physical, emotional, or sexual.

- Public humiliation.

- A failure.

- A bankruptcy.

- Poor performance academically or in sports.

DISCOVERY CHECKLIST

Do you respond out of a rejection-based personality? The list of questions below is designed to help you uncover rejection-based responses and lifestyles. Take your time as you prayerfully read the list, and let the Holy Spirit speak to your heart. Now is the time to be honest with yourself. You are reading this book because you are trying to understand rejection and find God's path to emotional healing. Answering these questions truthfully will help you learn more about yourself and help you more effectively minister to others. As you read the questions, put a check mark beside those things that trouble you.

☐ Do you have a fear of people's opinion of you?

☐ Are you a perfectionist?

☐ Are you frustrated with life?

☐ Are you abnormally anxious?

☐ Do you project a false sense of superiority?

☐ Are you suspicious of anything nice done for you?

☐ Do you have difficulty trusting God and others?

☐ Do you have difficulty understanding the love of God?

☐ Do you have difficulty showing love to others?

☐ Do you think that God cannot use you?

☐ Do you ask yourself, "How can God love me?"

☐ To "feel special" will you do extreme things like dangerous sports?

☐ Do you have severe bouts with depression and thoughts of suicide?

☐ Do you hide behind pets, books, hobbies, or work?

☐ Do you overemphasize material possessions? What about in dress or appearance?

☐ Do you have a dominating air or way about you?

☐ Do you have a critical spirit?

☐ Have you entered a self-imposed isolation from others?

☐ Do you feel empty and unfulfilled?

☐ Do you have a difficult time receiving love?

☐ Are there times when you don't want anyone to touch you?

☐ Do you value acceptance and hate correction?

☐ Do you have feelings of inferiority?

☐ Do you think that God does not love you as much as others?

☐ Do you dress to get attention?

☐ Do you have a fear of communicating your opinions?

☐ Do you detest being compared to others?

☐ Do you have uncontrolled bouts with pent up anger?

☐ Are there times when you feel undeserving?

☐ Do you feel that your lot in life is to suffer?

☐ Do you have a fear of failure?

☐ Are you a workaholic or overachiever?

☐ Do you take things too personally?

☐ Would you rather spend time with your pets or animals than people?

☐ Do you have a woe-is-me, gloomy view of life?

☐ Are you afraid to tell the truth about your feelings?

☐ Do you constantly fight discouragement?

☐ Are you harshly judgmental of others?

☐ Are you a faultfinder?

☐ Are you afraid of God?

☐ Are you always on the defensive?

☐ Do you have a problem relating to the opposite sex?

☐ Are you a procrastinator?

☐ Do you feel stupid, inferior, or self-conscious when around other people?

☐ Do you resent and hold bitterness toward others?

☐ Do you feel like you need to seek attention from others?

☐ Do you feel like you can never measure up to others?

☐ Are you driven to prove yourself to others?

☐ Are you troubled with constant mind traffic that gives you no rest?

☐ Do you have a problem saying, 'No' when you know that you need to?

☐ Do you feel threatened by others?

☐ Do you attack those you love and don't understand why?

☐ Do you think that no one understands you?

☐ Are you drawn towards base people who seem to be more accepting of you, yet do nothing to bring stability in your life?

☐ Are you sometimes introverted and at other times extroverted?

☐ Do you avoid being involved in group activities?

☐ Do you try to fit in with the crowd but never feel that you belong?

The checklist above is provided only to stir your thinking and allow the Holy Spirit reveal some of the root causes of why you feel the way you do. Once we recognize rejection, then we can begin the healing and rebuilding process. If you checked several of the items on the list, perhaps you are having difficulty with rejection. Don't worry – I have great news for you. Jesus is the answer to all your problems. He understands you better than you understand yourself. He has offered us a way of escape. His Word will teach you what to do. There is hope for you! There is life after rejection. In the next chapter, we will learn how Samuel handled rejection.

APERÇU

Everyone comes face-to-face with rejection. It is a part of everyday life.

We can't avoid rejection because we can't control the way people feel about us.

The negative feelings rejection causes stem from an improper internalization of various events.

Rejection is the feeling (internalization) that we are not valued or accepted.

When we do not feel accepted we must learn how to deal with the negative feelings that go with rejection.

Chapter 4

MINISTERIAL REJECTION

Everyone in ministry has faced rejection. I remember the negative feelings that bombarded my mind the first time someone got up and walked out of a service while I was preaching. It was a painful experience and forced me to deal with the spirit of rejection. I took heart when I understood the Gospel of Jesus Christ is the most accepted and rejected message in history. Every minister of the Gospel must quickly learn that it is not they but Christ who is being rejected. The prophet

> When you are hit with feelings of rejection it is important not to internalize those feelings.

Samuel faced strong feelings of rejection. Let's look at his ministry and how he overcame those feelings. The first mention of Samuel is when his mother Hannah promised God that if He would grant her a son she would give that son back to Him as a Nazarite (1 Samuel 1:11). Soon after her vow Hannah produced a child and named him Samuel. After weaning Samuel, Hannah, with her husband Elkanah, delivered the young child to Shilo, where Samuel was left in the care of Eli the high priest. After that Hannah and Elkanah visited their son Samuel only once each year (1 Samuel 2:19). Samuel never returned to his home in Ramah as a child. Sometimes I wonder if Samuel felt the least bit rejected when his parents left him with Eli. We may never know. Nevertheless, years later we find Samuel facing feelings of rejection in his ministry. Let's take a look.

Samuel was displeased with the Israelites because they asked for a king to govern them. The heathen nations around Israel had kings and the children of

Israel wanted to have a similar form of government. In short, Samuel felt rejected. But Samuel did what we should do when we face rejection. Samuel took those feelings to the Lord in prayer. The Lord was faithful to answer Samuel, and help the prophet put the rejection into perspective.

> "Hearken to the voice of the people in all that they say unto thee: for they have not rejected you, but they have rejected me, that I should not reign over them" (1 Samuel 8:7).

Like many of us, Samuel felt the people of God had rejected him when they turned away from the counsel of God. People who work in ministry constantly face this type of rejection. When you are hit with feelings of rejection it is important not to internalize those feelings. To internalize means to take the rejection personally by making it your own.

Again, Samuel's response to the feelings of rejection from the people was to take it to God in prayer. That is always the proper response. Scripture declares,

> "Casting all your care on him; for he careth for you" (1 Peter 5:7).

In responding to Samuel's prayer, the Lord pointed to the root of the prophet's feelings. The Lord let him know the Israelite's rebellion was at the heart of the rejection. Often prophets and prophetic people face a titanic battle with rejection. Prophets are the most spiritually sensitive of all the five-fold ascension gifts, but they must understand that it is the Lord Himself who is being rejected and not them. The instrument for a release of the spirit of rejection against Samuel was rebellion against God's authority and His divine right to rule (govern) the people.

ABANDONMENT AND REJECTION

The people's rejection of God caused them to abandon Samuel. Rejection and abandonment travel together. The Lord declared, "I brought them up out of Egypt even to this day, wherewith they have forsaken me, and served other gods, so do they also unto thee" (1 Samuel 8:8). The English Word forsaken stems from the Hebrew Word *azab* meaning to:

- Depart.

- Leave.

- Desert.

- Forsake.

- Neglect.

- Abandon.

Those who act out of rejection desert and abandon those who love them the most. God told Samuel to tell the people, who chose to abandon and reject Him for another, what life would be like for them when they had another king.

"And he said, This will be the manner of the king that will reign over you: He will take your sons, and appoint them for himself, for his chariots, and to be his horsemen; and some shall run before his chariots. And he will appoint him captains over thousands, and captains over fifties; and will set them to ear his ground, and to reap his harvest, and to make his instruments of war, and instruments of his chariots. And he will take your daughters to be confectionaries, and to be cooks, and to be bakers. And he will take your fields, and your vineyards, and your oliveyards, even the best of them, and give them to his servants. And he will take the tenth of your seed, and of your vineyards, and give to his officers, and to his servants. And he will take your menservants, and your maidservants, and your goodliest young men, and your asses, and put them to his work. He will take the tenth of your sheep: and you shall be his servants" (1 Samuel 8:11-17).

From this text we make a discovery: A person with rejection who refuses to submit to the rule of God will lose the liberty he takes for granted and exchange it for the control and lordship of another.

ACCEPTANCE FROM THE WRONG PEOPLE

It is common to see someone with the spirit of rejection fail to appreciate those who love them. It is just as common for people suffering from rejection to fail to recognize the graciousness of their true friends and sincere relatives. I have seen them reject their godly friends only to be controlled and dominated by self-serving manipulators such as Jezebel, Ahab, and Balaam. The Lord stressed over and over to the Israelites the new king "will take." The English words to take stems from the Greek word *laqach*, meaning to:

- Lay-hold of.

- Seize.

- Carry away.

- Procure to himself.

- Capture.

- Remove.

> People suffering with rejection want to feel accepted by the wrong people.

Sadly, even after Samuel pleaded with the people to reconsider their request they "refused to obey the voice of Samuel." The children of Israel no longer wanted to depend on God's Word or a life of faith. They rejected Him because they wanted a king over them like all the nations" (1 Samuel 8:19). Just as the Israelites wanted a king so they could be like other nations, people suffering with rejection also have a tendency to welcome the acceptance of the wrong people. Israel exchanged its all-sufficient King for a flawed human who would bring trouble on the nation.

Samuel handled the rejection properly – he did not take their rejection personally. Samuel did not internalize his feelings. The truth that helped Samuel press through rejection was his understanding that the people were not rejecting him – they were rejecting God. When you have God's acceptance, man's rejection is irrelevant.

In the next chapter we will look at the rejection that David faced and how he overcame it.

APERÇU

Samuel felt the people were rejecting him but in reality they were rejecting God.

When hit with feelings of rejection it is important not to internalize those feelings. To internalize means to take the rejection personally and make it your own.

A refusal to submit to the rule (government) of the Lord Jesus Christ and His Word is the instrument for the spirit of rejection.

People who act out of rejection desert and abandon those who love them the most.

The person with rejection who refuses to submit to the rule of God will lose the liberty that he takes for granted and exchange it for the control and lordship of another.

People suffering with rejection do not appreciate those who love them.

People suffering with rejection want to feel accepted by the wrong people.

Chapter 5

A FATHER'S REJECTION

If there is anyone in the Word of God who understood the pain of rejection, surely it was King David. Of all lives recorded in the Word of God, David is one of the most fascinating and inspiring. There are so many aspects of his life and faith that we can relate to on a personal level. Even though he seemed to be a stalwart man of steel and strength, he was also sensitive and tender. David is most remembered as the young lad who slew Goliath and became the champion of Israel.

As we study his testimony, however, we discover that his family life was far from perfect. As a matter of fact, his family life was a mess. It was totally dysfunctional. Many times throughout David's life he faced rejection's strong pillar. We can learn from David because he managed to find the strength in God to overcome. Despite David's many flaws, we can glean from this man who "was after God's own heart" (Acts 13:22). His life serves as continuing encouragement to people who suffer the pain of rejection.

In this chapter, we look at the times when David was rejected and how he overcame feelings that accompanied the hurtful acts. David was rejected by:

- His natural father, Jesse.

- His brothers.

- King Saul, his spiritual father.

- His wife Michal.

- His close friend.

- His son Absalom.

We first discover David when God sends the Prophet Samuel to anoint a new king to succeed the disobedient Saul. God sent Samuel to Bethlehem to anoint one of Jesse's sons as the future king of Israel. Let's take a look.

> "And the Lord said to Samuel, How long wilt thou mourn for Saul, seeing I have rejected him from reigning over Israel? fill thine horn with oil, and go, I will send thee to Jesse the Bethlehemite: for I have provided me a king among his sons" (1 Samuel 16:1).

After he arrived at Bethlehem, Samuel invited Jesse and his sons to attend a special sacrifice to the Lord. Samuel didn't tell Jesse the Lord sent him to anoint a king, yet it must have been an honor for Jesse's family to be personally invited to this sacred gathering. For his part, Samuel must have been impressed when he looked on Jesse's seven fine looking sons. They were tall, handsome and strong. There was Eliab, Abinadab, Shammah, and four others who stood before the prophet of God. Surely, he thought, the Lord's anointed was among them. Let's take a look at the Scriptures that offer some insight into this meeting; a meeting at which David was noticeably absent. Samuel said to Jesse,

"I am come to sacrifice unto the Lord: sanctify yourselves, and come with me to the sacrifice. And he sanctified Jesse and his sons, and called them to the sacrifice. And it came to pass, when they were come, that he looked on Eliab, and said, Surely the Lord's anointed is before him. But the Lord said to Samuel, Look not on his countenance, or on the height of his stature; because I have refused him: for the Lord seeth not as man seeth; for man looketh on the outward appearance, but the Lord looketh on the heart. Then Jesse called Abinadab, and made him pass before Samuel. And he said, Neither hath the Lord chosen this. Then Jesse made Shammah to pass by. And he said, Neither hath the Lord chosen this. Again, Jesse made seven of his sons to pass before Samuel. And Samuel said unto Jesse, The Lord hath not chosen these" (1 Samuel 16:5-10).

Samuel was prepared to fulfill his God-given mission but the Lord made it clear the young men who stood before him were not to be anointed the next king of Israel. Samuel must have been perplexed, until God explained He "looketh on the heart" and not on the outward appearance. Knowing the Lord had said the next king was among Jesse's sons, Samuel then asked Jesse if he had any more children.

> "And Samuel said to Jesse, Are here all thy children? And he said, There remaineth yet the youngest, and, behold, he keepeth the sheep. And Samuel said to Jesse, Send and fetch him: for we will not sit down till he come hither. And he sent, and brought him in. Now he was ruddy, and withal of a beautiful countenance, and goodly to look to. And the Lord said, Arise, anoint him: for this is he. Then Samuel took the horn of oil, and anointed him in the midst of his brethren: and the spirit of the Lord came on David from that day forward. So Samuel rose up, and went to Ramah" (1 Samuel 16:11-13).

Isn't it interesting that Jesse did not make sure David was there, with his other sons, to meet the prophet? It would have been a simple matter to get someone else to tend the sheep so David could be part of this special occasion. After all, how often did a prophet come to town and invite the entire family to a special service?

> **David's father, brothers, King Saul, his wife, his close friend, and his son Absalom, all rejected him.**

Samuel insisted Jesse call his missing son, and waited for the youngest to arrive. As soon as Samuel saw David, the Lord spoke saying, "Arise and anoint him in the midst of his brethren." David was God's chosen vessel. Although the other family members did not recognize the value of this young lad, God did. The Bible tells us the Spirit of the Lord came on David from that day forward.

These events cause us to ask some important questions. Why didn't Jesse include David in the meeting? Could it be that he didn't consider him important enough to meet with the prophet? What was David's relationship with his older brothers? What about his father? Where was David's mother? Had she died giving birth to David? Was David received or rejected by his siblings? After the Lord refused to anoint David's brothers, did they feel rejected?

Regardless of your conclusions, it's important to remember this: God looks on the heart of man when He makes His decision to anoint someone. It is also important to note that one must keep his heart right before the Lord regardless of everyone else's opinion of his value.

From David's experience, we learn that everyone is important to the Lord. Even when it appears that your parents have rejected or left you out, rest assured God has not left you out. In fact, our Lord will do whatever it takes to reach you. Our God has not rejected us but has received us. He does not look on the outward appearance as man looks. He looks at our hearts. Great is our God!

In the next chapter we learn how to deal with sibling rejection.

APERÇU

David's father, brothers, King Saul, his wife, his close friend, and his son, Absalom, all rejected him.

Jesse did not invite David to the meeting with the prophet Samuel, who God sent to anoint the next king of Israel.

God looks on the heart of man when He makes His decision to anoint someone.

Even when it appears your parents have rejected or left you out, rest assured God has not left you out.

God looks on the heart of man when He makes His decision to anoint someone.

Chapter 6

SIBLING REJECTION

Sibling rivalry exists to some extent between all siblings. Many times sibling rivalry, however, turns into all-out abuse. Indeed, sibling rivalry sets children up to deal with issues of rejection. Let's take a look at David's relationship with his brothers to see if his brothers were jealous of the young lad. We can discern the attitudes of David's siblings toward him by how they treated him on the day he defeated Goliath.

As the chronicle goes, one day the Philistines assembled their armies to battle against Israel. The

Philistines stood on one side of a mountain. Israel stood on the other side. Only a valley separated the archrivals. The Philistines presented their champion warrior named Goliath of Gath. His height was six cubits and a span. (That's over nine feet!) As Goliath approached the armies of Israel he mocked and challenged them. His voice was heard throughout the camp of Israel taunting,

> "Why did you come out to set your battle in array? Am not I a Philistine, and you servants to Saul? Choose you a man for you, and let him come down to me. If he be able to fight with me, and to kill me, then will we be your servants: but if I prevail against him, and kill him, then shall you be our servants, and serve us." As if those words weren't clear enough, Goliath threw down the gauntlet, saying, "I defy the armies of Israel this day; give me a man that we may fight together" (1 Samuel 17:8-10).

Goliath was a formidable looking foe. The Word of God says, "When Saul and all Israel heard the words of the Philistine, they were dismayed, and greatly afraid" (1 Samuel 17:11). But God had a young boy whom He had prepared for such a time. As we know, his name was David, the son of Jesse.

David had three brothers serving in King Saul's army. Their names were Eliab, the firstborn. Next to him there was Abinadab. The third was Shammah (1 Samuel 17:13). Knowing his sons were gathered at the battlefield, Jesse sent the young David to his brothers with gifts of food. Jesse also directed David to find out how his brothers were faring (1 Samuel 17:17-18). As David approached the battlefield he heard the railing voice of Goliath, the champion of the Philistines. This so stirred young David that he declared among the camp, "Who is this uncircumcised Philistine, that he should defy the armies of the living God?" (1 Samuel 17:26).

David's older brother Eliab offered a frigid response to David. With utter scorn and contempt, Eliab asked David, "Why are you here? Where did you leave those few sheep?" Eliab did not receive or respect his little brother. In fact, he was angry. Eliab despised David all the more for showing up to the battle. It seems Eliab didn't want David anywhere near him.

David was severally rejected by his family. Could it be they remembered the visit from the Prophet Samuel who rejected them and anointed David to become king over Israel? Eliab continued badgering David: "I know your pride and the naughtiness of your heart. Did you just come to the battle to watch?" (1 Samuel 17:28).

> **What others think about you is not as important as what God thinks about you.**

Eliab falsely accused David of having deceitful motives, pride, and apathy, none of which was an accurate description.

It must have been painful for David to be rejected by his oldest brother. After all, the younger sibling often looks up to and admires the older brother. David's reaction to Eliab's accusations came in the form of a question: "What have I done now?" David's question suggests his brothers were riding his case for some reason or another regularly.

If rejection has stung you, you must decide this: What others think of you is not as important as what God thinks of you. David's response to Eliab is something rejected people can learn from. David asked his brother, "Is there not a cause? And he turned from him toward another" (1 Samuel 17:29-30). Many of us will face false accusations from family members. David turned away from the rejection of his brother and stated his cause. Then he prophesied his future. Let's read this Scripture.

"And he turned from him toward another, and spake after the same manner: and the people answered him again after the former manner. And when the words were heard which David spake, they rehearsed them before Saul: and he sent for him. And David said to Saul, Let no man's heart fail because of him; thy servant will go and fight with this Philistine. And Saul said to David, You are not able to go against this Philistine to fight with him: for you are but a youth, and he a man of war from his youth. And David said unto Saul, Thy servant kept his father's sheep, and there came a lion, and a bear, and took a lamb out of the flock: And I went out after him, and smote him, and delivered it out of his mouth: and when he arose against me, I caught him by his beard, and smote him, and slew him. Thy servant slew both the lion and the bear: and this uncircumcised Philistine shall be as one of them, seeing he hath defied the armies of the living God. David said moreover, The Lord that delivered me out of the paw of the lion, and out of the paw of the bear, he will deliver me out of the hand of this Philistine.

And Saul said to David, Go, and the Lord be with thee" (1 Samuel 17:30-37).

Instead of taking his brother's accusations to heart, David focused on the big picture. There wasn't time for a self-centered pity-party. God's people were being challenged. David simply turned away from his brother's false accusations. Like David, people who face rejection must discipline themselves to turn away from false accusations and pity-parties. David never considered his brother's comments. If he had, he never would have defeated Goliath. God had prepared David for that moment in time. A new champion was about to be revealed to Israel. But he had to overcome rejection before he walked off the battlefield in victory. David took three clear steps to overcome the power of rejection. These steps are important insights for us. Let's review:

1. David turned away from his brother's false accusations and unto God's purpose.

2. David stated his cause and reason for living when he said, "Who is this uncircumcised Philistine that would challenge the armies of the living God?"

3. David prophesied his future by decreeing, "Thy servant slew both the lion and the bear: and this uncircumcised Philistine shall be as one of them, seeing he hath defied the armies of the living God."

These three actions are powerful tools of freedom to those who suffer from rejection. Are you ready to turn away, state your cause, and prophesy your future? Are you ready for life after rejection? In the next chapter we learn that rejection by a spouse can be one of the most painful events in life.

APERÇU

Many times sibling rivalry turns into all-out abuse. Indeed, sibling rivalry sets children up to deal with issues of rejection.

David's brothers did not receive or respect him.

David's brother falsely accused him of having deceitful motives, pride, and apathy, none of which was an accurate description.

What others think about you is not as important as what God thinks about you.

David did not take his brother's accusations to heart. Instead, he focused on the big picture.

David took three key steps to overcoming rejection. He turned away from false accusations and pity-parties. He stated his cause, his reason for living. And he prophesied his future.

Chapter 7

SPOUSAL REJECTION

When a spouse rejects you it can be one of the
most painful events in life. Some have equated
its pain to the death of a loved one. In this chapter,
we will look at how David responded when his wife,
Michal, rejected him.

DAVID AND MICHAL

David entered a deep experience with the Lord on the
day he moved the ark of God's presence from Obed-
edom's house into the city of Jerusalem. It was such an

incredible event that David "danced before the Lord with all his might" (2 Samuel 6:14). How awesome it was to finally have God's presence in the city. Just picture it. Everyone must have been leaning out of their windows shouting, "Glory to God in the highest!" All except one, that is. When Michal, David's wife, saw her husband leaping and dancing in the streets, her response was different.

> "And as the ark of the Lord came into the city of David, Michal Saul's daughter looked through a window, and saw king David leaping and dancing before the Lord; and she despised (bazah) him in her heart" (2 Samuel 6:16).

The word despise stems from the Hebrew word *bazah*, meaning "to view as worthless." The spirit of rejection tries to make people feel as if they have no value; that they are worthless. Let's look at how this spirit set David up for disappointment.

After the priests set the ark in its proper place, David offered burnt offerings and peace offerings to the Lord. Then, he blessed the people in the name of the Lord of Hosts. What an anointed service that must have been! In this faith-filled and joyous time, David blessed the people with bread and drink. When the festivities were over, he left to bless his own home. Sadly, David is about to be rejected by his wife Michal. Let's read what she said.

"Then David returned to bless his household. And Michal the daughter of Saul came out to meet David, and said, How glorious was the king of Israel today, who uncovered himself today in the eyes of the handmaids of his servants, as one of the vain fellows shamelessly uncovereth himself!" (2 Samuel 6:20)

Michal, Saul's daughter, rejected David's response to the Lord. She found his manner or expression of worship embarrassing. Consider this: Saul is a type of the religious spirit. Michal, his daughter, is a prophetic type of the religious spirit's fruit. Religion never understands heartfelt expression of God's love or man's response to it. Religion is a thief of monumental proportions. (For more information on the dangerous spirit of religion, what it looks like, how it acts and why it is targeting born-again believers like you, pick up my book *30 Pieces of Silver*.)

The moment Michal rebuked David, he was face-to-face with the spirit of rejection. His wife had counted him as worthless. How David responds will decide his

> When a spouse rejects you it can be one of the most painful events in life. Some have equated its pain to the death of a loved one.

future. Will he submit to his religious wife's disdain and rebuke? Will he try to keep peace in his home by compromising his faith? Will he try to meet Michal halfway? Let's learn how we, too, can resist rejection through the example of David's response to Michal rejecting him.

"And David said unto Michal, It was before the Lord, which chose me before thy father, and before all his house, to appoint me ruler over the people of the Lord, over Israel: therefore will I play before the Lord. And I will yet be more vile than thus, and will be base in mine own sight: and of the maidservants which thou hast spoken of, of them shall I be had in honor. Therefore Michal the daughter of Saul had no child unto the day of her death." (2 Samuel 6:21-23).

This Scripture teaches us two important truths about resisting the spirit of rejection. First, David did not submit to his wife's false accusations. Remember, we are not who rejection says that we are. We are who Christ says we are. David did not compromise for peace. He held fast to the truth. So the first truth is this: to successfully resist rejection, we can never compromise our faith in God.

Second, David decreed his position in the kingdom. He declared, "It was the Lord who chose me ruler." We, too, must remember that we are seated in heavenly places in Christ Jesus. Because of our position in Christ, we are seated far away from the control of the spirit of rejection. We are above and not beneath! What He has done for us nobody can take away.

"And hath raised us up together, and made us sit together in heavenly places in Christ Jesus" (Ephesians 2:6).

David responded to Michal by saying, "Therefore I will play before the Lord and become more vile (Hebrew *qalal*, meaning insignificant) than that." In other words, "If my expression of great joy looked trifling, insignificant, or below me, I will lower myself even further in God's presence." David teaches us a powerful truth with that statement. The lesson is this: humility is a great weapon against the spirit of rejection. Humility is the opposite of pride or self-assertion. A humble person recognizes that his life is not his own.

"What? know ye not that your body is the temple of the Holy Ghost which is in you, which ye have of God, and *you are not your own?* For ye are bought with a price: therefore glorify God in your body, and in your spirit, which are God's" (1 Corinthians 6:19-20, Italics added).

Severe marital problems and divorce are a leading cause of rejection. Many divorced people find it difficult to begin life again after divorce. They often struggle with feelings of failure and low self-esteem. It should also be pointed out that rejection is passed along throughout the family. Not only did Michal reject David. He also rejected her. Seemingly from this day forward, David and Michal refused to sleep with each other. As a result she bore him no children. I am sure that not birthing children negatively affected Michal throughout her life.

APERÇU

When a spouse rejects you it can be one of the most painful events in life. Some have equated its pain to the death of a loved one.

Successfully resisting rejection means never compromising our faith in God.

If you are faced with rejection, decree your position in the Kingdom (Ephesians 2:6). Our position in Christ has seated us far away from the control of the spirit of rejection.

The word despise, Hebrew, *bazah*, means "to view as worthless."

Religion is a thief of monumental proportions.

Severe marital problems and divorce are a leading cause of rejection.

Chapter 8

REJECTION BY CHILDREN

Absalom was David's third-born son. He was born to Maacha, the daughter of Tholmai, King of Gessur. The Bible offers an image of Absalom as an especially handsome young man with a full head of bushy black hair. David must have been proud of him. But he wasn't proud of all Absalom did. We see the first hint of an evil design in Absalom's heart when he murders his older brother, Amnon, for raping his sister Tamar. Apparently, David heard about the rape but failed to punish the crime. Absalom took justice into his own hands. Sometimes when there is serious sin in families, those with authority ignore what's going on or do nothing to stop the offenses. Somehow they think not saying anything will protect the family from being shamed or dishonored. This creates an environment in which Satan loves to work.

TAMAR'S RAPE AND REJECTION

Let's step back a moment and read the wicked testimony of Tamar's rape and rejection – and its aftermath. David's failure to take action releases a tragic series of events that affects the entire family.

"And when she had brought them unto him to eat, he took hold of her, and said unto her, Come lie with me, my sister. And she answered him, Nay, my brother, do not force me; for no such thing ought to be done in Israel: do not thou this folly. And I, whither shall I cause my shame to go? and as for thee, thou shalt be as one of the fools in Israel. Now therefore, I pray thee, speak unto the king; for he will not withhold me from thee. Howbeit he would not hearken unto her voice: but, being stronger than she, forced her, and lay with her. Then Amnon hated her exceedingly; so that the hatred wherewith he hated her was greater than the love wherewith he had loved her. And Amnon said unto her, Arise, be gone. And she said unto him, There is no cause: this evil in sending me away is greater than the other that thou didst unto me. But he would not hearken unto her. Then he called his servant that ministered unto him, and said, Put now this woman out from me, and bolt the door after her. And she had a garment of divers colors upon her: for with such robes were the king's daughters that were virgins appareled. Then his servant brought her out, and bolted the door after her. And Tamar put ashes on her head, and rent her garment of divers colors that was on her, and laid her hand on her head, and went on crying" (2 Samuel 13:11-19).

After Amnon, Tamar's half brother, committed his incestuous crime, he could not stand the evil of his own actions. He rejects Tamar, commanding his servants to throw her out and bolt the door, locking her out of his presence. Tamar left the house devastated by the incident. She fled to her brother Absalom.

Sadly, this pattern of sexual abuse and rejection still occurs all too often in families today. Throughout my years of ministry, I have met people who were molested by a relative or a close friend of the family. Nonaction to protect a family member who is suffering from any type of abuse releases an air of mistrust, which breeds rejection. Some of life's most painful rejection events come from childhood experiences. In fact, when you suffer rejection in your early years it can and often does set the tone for your

> **Rejection suffered in the early years often sets the tone for a person's entire life.**

entire life. Whenever a parent, grandparent, or someone we hold in esteem is not there for us, feelings of being unloved, unworthy, useless, defenseless, or insignificant can develop. The good news is there is life after rejection if we choose to deal with it God's way and move on. Unfortunately, David and his family did not deal with Tamar's rape God's way.

ABSALOM RESPONDS TO TAMAR

"And Absalom her brother said unto her, Hath Amnon thy brother been with thee? But hold now thy peace, my sister: he is thy brother; regard not this thing. So Tamar remained desolate (devastated) in her brother Absalom's house" (2 Samuel 13:20).

Absalom saw his sister Tamar's distress. When he questioned her he discovered Amnon had molested her. Absalom was sure dad, King David, would punish the offender, but David did nothing to correct the crime.

Absalom must have viewed David's refusal to get involved in this family matter as a weakness and an excuse to take matters into his own hands. After all, how could his father ignore a rape in the house? What about Tamar's feelings of abandonment? How do you think she felt about this? What about the inaction of her father to stand up for her honor? How could she not have experienced the pains of rejection? Not only did her brother sexually violate her, her father refused to get involved.

DAVID DOESN'T ACT

David was not without feeling in the wake of his daughter's rape. Scripture reveals David was furious with Amnon for abusing Tamar. Still, he did nothing to bring correction or justice. Why? Could it be possible that rejection was causing him to hide from further investigation?

> "But when king David heard of all these things, he was very wroth (furious)" (2 Samuel 13:21).

David's story teaches what we refuse to deal with today will come back to haunt us tomorrow.

Wroth, yes, but there is no biblical evidence that David ever consoled his daughter Tamar or dealt with Amnon on this issue. A parent's abandonment or inaction can lead to feelings of rejection. Guilt and shame of having been abused is another wide avenue of rejection. Satan looks for any way he can to keep rejection working in our families because he comes to steal, kill and destroy.

David's own rejection experiences opened a door for fear, which hindered his involvement in the family crisis. The bottom line is this: David did not handle his daughter's rape correctly. He didn't handle it at all. Not only was David the king, he was also Dad. But where was Dad? And why wasn't he Tamar's advocate? Because of rejection David:

- Ignored a serious issue.

- Passed rejection on to his daughter.

- Was afraid to confront a painful family situation.

- Did not exercise his authority as head and priest over his household.

- Abandoned Tamar in her time of need.

- Lost the respect of his son Absalom.

Eventually, David's past rejection experiences hindered him from getting involved with this painful family problem. Rejection severely hindered David's judgment. Often people suffering from rejection will not confront people they love because they don't want to risk uncovering other hurts and wounds they buried deep within. Rejection will cause you to hurt others who need your help. David's story teaches what we refuse to deal with today will come back to haunt us tomorrow.

BIRTHING OF BITTERNESS

For two years Absalom carried hatred in his heart toward his brother Amnon. David's inaction opened the door to a root of bitterness in Absalom's heart. Absalom was bitter against David. Then, one day Absalom decided to take actions of his own. He displayed his cunning, inviting David and all his brothers to a sheep shearing festival in a valley called Baalhazor in the land of Ephraim (2 Samuel 13:23). The first clip of the flocks was ordained for the priests (Deuteronomy 18:4) and the sacredness of the feast made it difficult for any member of the tribal family to absent himself.

"Now Absalom had commanded his servants, saying, Mark ye now when Amnon's heart is merry with wine, and when I say to you, Smite Amnon; then kill him, fear not: have not I commanded you? Be courageous, and be

valiant. And the servants of Absalom did unto
Amnon as Absalom had commanded. Then all
the king's sons arose, and every man got him up
on his mule, and fled" (2 Samuel 13:28-29).

David declined the invitation, but Absalom's
brothers, including Amnon, attended. Absalom directed
his servants to watch Amnon and kill him when he got
drunk. Absalom's servants did as he commanded. It is
amazing to learn that bitterness (long held resentment)
can give birth to calculated murder as we see Absalom
had his own flesh and blood brother killed.

> "And it came to pass, while they were in the way,
> that tidings came to David, saying, Absalom
> hath slain all the king's sons, and there is not
> one of them left. Then the king arose, and tare
> his garments, and lay on the earth; and all his
> servants stood by with their clothes rent. And
> Jonadab, the son of Shimeah David's brother,
> answered and said, Let not my Lord suppose
> that they have slain all the young men the
> king's sons; for Amnon only is dead: for by
> the appointment of Absalom this hath been
> determined from the day that he forced his

sister Tamar. Now therefore let not my Lord
the king take the thing to his heart, to think
that all the king's sons are dead: for Amnon
only is dead" (2 Samuel 13:30-33).

This family tragedy deeply wounded David. Family
turmoil is a common cause of rejection. Indeed,
rejection flourishes amid family conflict. Think about
it. David had lost Amnon, whom Absalom's servants
murdered in cold blood. Tamar was still estranged
and now Absalom would be lost, too. David probably
wondered how one of his sons could take the life of his
brother? How grieved he must have been. The Bible
reveals that people who were close to David found him
in mourning everyday. Even as I pen these words, I can
feel a measure of his pain for his daughter and both
of his sons. I wonder what the other family members
were thinking.

> "But Absalom fled. And the young man that
> kept the watch lifted up his eyes, and looked,
> and, behold, there came much people by the
> way of the hill side behind him. And Jonadab
> said to the king, Behold, the king's sons come:
> as thy servant said, so it is. And it came to pass,
> as soon as he had made an end of speaking, that,

behold, the king's sons came, and lifted up their voice and wept: and the king also and all his servants wept very sore" (2 Samuel 13:34-36).

ABSALOM FLEES TO GRANDFATHER'S HOUSE

Absalom escaped his father's anger by seeking refuge in his maternal grandfather's home in Gessur. There he hoped to remain until the grief of his father died out. Then, he hoped, he might be forgiven and recalled to the royal court. But David did not relent so quickly. Only after three years of banishment and through the intervention of Joab, David's nephew and trusted general, was Absalom allowed to return to the city. But Absalom was still not allowed to enter the king's presence.

David's pain did not allow him to speak with Absalom. So the rejection cycle continues as David began rejecting Absalom. People suffering with rejection often refuse to deal with uncomfortable situations by drawing into themselves and ignoring what's going on around them. We can never ignore the pain. Stored up pain will build a rejection-based personality that refuses to let us do the right thing. Remember the house that rejection builds? If David would have spoken to Absalom as a loving father, repented of his own sin of neglect and failings while still holding Absalom accountable he may have stopped the tragic events that would soon follow.

ABSALOM
RETURNS TO JERUSALEM

At some point, after Absalom returned to Jerusalem, he clearly won the confidence of his father and was restored to his former princely dignity. Still, even after 40 years Absalom held a grudge against his father for not dealing with his sister's rape. Bitterness had entered his heart and he had no respect for his father. In fact, Absalom refused to honor his father as king. Once Absalom had the opportunity, he began undermining his father's credibility among the people. He slowly and methodically set out to steal the hearts of the Israelites, turning them away from David and to himself. He created an undercurrent of discontent among the people by making them feel David was neglecting their needs. Satan looks for every opportunity of hurt, pain, or unforgiveness to orchestrate our demise.

ABSALOM BETRAYS DAVID

Absalom was setting David up for a major betrayal. Absalom lied to his father, telling him he was going to Hebron to fulfill a self-imposed vow. Instead, he left and incited a conspiracy against David (2 Samuel 15:12). Absalom began to unite hundreds of men that were willing to overthrow his father's rule.

"See, I will tarry in the plain of the wilderness, until there come Word from you to certify me. Zadok therefore and Abiathar carried the ark of God again to Jerusalem: and they tarried there. And David went up by the ascent of mount Olivet, and wept as he went up, and had his head covered, and he went barefoot: and all the people that was with him covered every man his head, and they went up, weeping as they went up. And one told David, saying, Ahithophel is among the conspirators with Absalom. And David said, O Lord, I pray thee, turn the counsel of Ahithophel into foolishness. And it came to pass, that when David was come to the top of the mount, where he worshipped God, behold, Hushai the Archite came to meet him with his coat rent, and earth on his head: To whom David said, If thou passest on with me, then thou shalt be a burden to me" (2 Samuel 15:28-33).

DAVID ESCAPES
THE COUP D' ETAT

When David got word of Absalom's caudate he fled for his life. The Word declares that he left Jerusalem in tears (2 Samuel 15:30). What a tragic day this must have been. Can you imagine one of your children going to such great lengths to destroy you and your ministry? David must have asked himself many times, "Where did I go wrong with this boy?"

Absalom was full of bitterness, treachery, deceit, pride, arrogance, and sedition. These were the motivators behind his betrayal of his father who loved him dearly. How did David make it through this historic day? To be forced to leave everything he had worked so hard to gain must have sorely worn against his heart.

In the face of all of this, the Word says that David submitted his life to God and began to worship Him (2 Samuel 15:32). I can only imagine David's prayer as the sun was setting on the dark events of that day. Perhaps his prayer went something like this,

> "The Lord is my shepherd; I shall not want. He maketh me to lie down in green pastures: he leadeth me beside the still waters. He restoreth my soul: he leadeth me in the paths of righteousness for his name's sake. Yea, though I walk through the valley of the shadow of death, I will fear no evil: for thou art with me; thy rod and thy staff they comfort me. Thou preparest a table before me in the presence of mine enemies: thou anointest my head with oil; my cup runneth over. Surely goodness and mercy shall follow me all the days of my life: and I will dwell in the house of the Lord forever" (Psalm 23).

This is a good prayer for people struggling with rejection because the only way to combat rejection is to gain a strong understanding of your position in Christ.

Now consider this: Not only did David's son reject and betray him, hundreds of people who were once loyal to his kingdom also followed Absalom in his treachery. David had fought many wars so Israel could live in peace. Now people who once praised him for his mighty deeds and gallantry turned their backs on him and joined a traitor.

As the story continues, we find out Absalom's treachery against his father did not succeed. Joab killed Absalom while his hair was caught in the fork of a low hanging tree branch. Absalom couldn't escape and met his fate that day.

> "Then said Joab, I may not tarry thus with thee. And he took three darts in his hand, and thrust them through the heart of Absalom, while he was yet alive in the midst of the oak" (2 Samuel 18:14).

When David heard about Absalom's death he was deeply grieved. "

> And the king was much moved, and went up to the chamber over the gate, and wept: and as he went, thus he said, O my son Absalom, my son, my son Absalom! Would God I had died for thee, O Absalom, my son, my son!" (2 Samuel 18:33)

DAVID'S UNCONTROLLABLE GRIEF

David did not handle his grief for Absalom properly amid his people. The uncontrollable grief in David's heart was obvious with every tear. You might say his cup was running over with grief. Rejection had hit its mark and taken him captive. Scripture teaches us that,

> "Word soon reached Joab that the king was weeping and mourning for Absalom. As the troops heard of the king's deep grief for his son, the joy of that day's victory was turned into deep sadness. They crept back into the city as though they were ashamed and had been beaten in battle. The king covered his face with his hands and kept on weeping, "O my son Absalom! O Absalom, my son, my son!" (2 Samuel 19:1-4 NLT)

CORRECTION IS PROOF OF SONSHIP

David's wasn't thinking of those who were witnessing his behavior. He was suffering intensely from deep and lingering pain in his heart for the loss of another son. God sent Joab, a trusted general who fought many battles alongside David, to correct him. David had to stop acting the way he was. Rejection was robbing the joy of victory from him and his men. Let's listen in to the uncomfortable event. The Bible reads,

"Then Joab went to the king's room and said to him, We saved your life today and the lives of your sons, your daughters, and your wives and concubines. Yet you act like this, making us feel ashamed, as though we had done something wrong. You seem to love those who hate you and hate those who love you (misplaced loyalty). You have made it clear today that we mean nothing to you. If Absalom had lived and all of us had died, you would be pleased. Now go out there and congratulate the troops, for I swear by the Lord that if you don't, not a single one of them will remain here tonight. Then you will be worse off than you have ever been. So the king went out and sat at the city gate, and as the news spread throughout the city that he was there, everyone went to him" (2 Samuel 19:5-8 NLT).

DAVID'S MISPLACED LOYALITY

David's uncontrollable grief and feelings of rejection caused him to misplace his loyalty. David was weeping over Absalom and should have been rejoicing in their victory. He was bound in self-centered anguish. Rejection had stolen his ability to see what was taking place around him and how his behavior was impacting others.

David found no sympathy from his old trusted friend, General Joab. Joab refused to pet David's flesh; rather he rebuked David for his pity-party and misplaced loyalty. It was vital that David express his appreciation to his men who had risked their lives to restore David to the throne. He could not afford to let his rejection rob the spirit of victory from his men.

Because of the house that rejection built, David was simply not acting right. His personality was malfunctioning. Joab would have failed to help David had he offered David what he wanted – soulish sympathy – rather than what he needed – good solid counsel.

I have seen people repeat this same mistake after a great victory. Instead of rejoicing in the success the Lord provided, they spoil the celebration with a display of woe-is-me. We can never let rejection stop us from doing the right thing. Rejection wants us to place our attention on the wrong things. Rejection misplaces our loyalty. If David had received the sympathy and soulish compassion he was looking for, he would have lost his kingdom despite his victory over Absalom's rebellion.

APERÇU

Some of life's most painful rejection events come from childhood experiences.

Rejection suffered in the early years often sets the tone for a person's entire life.

Feelings of being unloved, unworthy, useless, or insignificant can develop when a parent, grandparent, or someone we hold in esteem, rejects us.

When a parent abandons a child it can leave that child with feelings of rejection.

When a person is sexually abused, it becomes a major avenue for guilt, shame and rejection.

Family turmoil allows rejection to flourish.

People suffering with rejection often refuse to deal with uncomfortable situations. Instead, they draw into themselves and ignore what's going on around them.

Stored up pain will build a rejection-based personality that refuses to let you do the right thing.

If David would have spoken to Absalom as a loving father, repented of his own inabilities and sin of neglect while still holding Absalom accountable for his actions, he may have stopped the tragic events that followed.

David found no sympathy from Joab. He would not pet his flesh. Rather Joab rebuked David for his pity-party and misplaced loyalty.

Rejection wants us to place our attention on the wrong things.

If David had received the sympathy and soulish compassion he was looking for he would have lost his kingdom despite his victory over Absalom's rebellion.

Chapter 9

REJECTION BY CLOSE FRIENDS

Betrayal and abandonment run rampant in today's society. When someone close to you rejects you, it is painful. I've met many women who were abandoned by their fathers at a young age and many other women who were abandoned by their husbands later in life. Speaking for me, some who I thought were close friends forsook me without even so much as a good-bye. People who have been abandoned often feel empty, hopeless, and insecure. They view life, relationships, themselves, and their future with uncertainty. We must recognize that betrayal and abandonment are common weapons the enemy uses to inflict the pain of rejection.

DAVID AND AHITHOPHEL

David experienced the pain of betrayal and abandonment when his counsel and close friend Ahithophel, grandfather of Bathsheba, joined the revolt of his traitorous son Absalom (2 Samuel 15:12). David said, "Yea, mine own familiar friend, in whom I trusted, which did eat of my bread, hath lifted up his heel against me" (Psalms 41:9). Not only did David have to press through the pain of Absalom's betrayal, but now his most trusted companion also turned his back on him. David must have been crushed by this series of events, yet God gave him strength to continue. After searching the Scriptures, the following text best captures the anguish of betrayal and abandonment David felt.

"My heart is sore pained within me: and the terrors of death are fallen on me. Fearfulness and trembling are come upon me, and horror hath overwhelmed me. And I said, Oh that I had wings like a dove! For then would I fly away, and be at rest. Lo, then would I wander far off, and remain in the wilderness. Selah" (Psalms 55:4-7).

David was clearly hurt by the betrayal of his closest friend Ahithophel. Who wouldn't be? To be sure, David was "sore pained." That means there was a gut-wrenching grief inside him. He just wanted to "fly away." People suffering with rejection just want to escape pain by running or hiding. Just like David, they would rather "remain in the wilderness" than face life anymore.

> "For it was not an enemy that reproached me; then I could have borne it: neither was it he that hated me that did magnify himself against me; then I would have hid myself from him: But it was thou, a man mine equal, my guide, and mine acquaintance. We took sweet counsel together, and walked to the house of God in company" (Psalms 55:12-14).

Not only was Ahithophel David's close companion, they also went to church together. Just as church leaders have hurt their disciples, many disciples hurt one another. In fact, the Church is filled with born-again believers who have inflicted the pain of rejection on another. This should not be so.

> "He hath put forth his hands against such as be at peace with him: he hath broken his covenant. The words of his mouth were smoother than butter, but war was in his heart: his Words were softer than oil, yet were they drawn swords" (Psalms 55:20-21).

David laments that his friend violated his trust and friendship. He had broken their covenant because there was "war in his heart."

THREE KEYS TO FREEDOM

For all the anguish we find in this psalm, David also gives us valuable insight into how to deflect the pain of betrayal and abandonment. Let's look at the three keys that unlocked David's freedom. David proves again and again there is life after rejection.

> "Cast thy burden upon the Lord, and he shall sustain thee: he shall never suffer the righteous

to be moved. But thou, O God, shalt bring them down into the pit of destruction: bloody and deceitful men shall not live out half their days; but I will trust in thee" (Psalms 55:22-23).

First, David "cast his burden on the Lord." The Word cast is Hebrew *shalak*, meaning to:

- Throw.

- Hurl.

- Fling.

- Shed.

- Cast off.

Scripture tells us Jesus took our "weaknesses and bore our sicknesses" (Matthew 8:17). One of the most helpful prayers when someone hurts is this: "Lord I cast all my cares on you because I know that you care for me" (1 Peter 5:7).

Second, David confessed the Word of God over his life. He declared, "He will sustain me and never suffer the righteous to be moved (shaken)." The word sustain stems from the Hebrew word *kuwl*, meaning to:

- Hold-up.

- Nourish.

- Refresh.

- Support.

- Supply.

Next, David confessed that he didn't understand why all these things were happening to him but he boldly said, "Yet will I trust God." As painful as betrayal and abandonment are, we can still depend on Jesus to help us get through it all. People who face rejection must do what David did when he cried out to the Lord in prayer and declared God to be his refuge and his reason for living.

"Maschil of David; A Prayer when he was in the cave. I cried to the Lord with my voice; with my voice to the Lord did I make my supplication. I poured out my complaint before him; I showed before him my trouble. When my spirit was overwhelmed within me, then thou knewest my path. In the way wherein I walked have they privately laid a snare for me. I looked on my right hand, and beheld, but there was no man that would know me: refuge failed me; no man cared for my soul. I cried to thee, O Lord: I said, Thou art my refuge and my portion in the land of the living. Attend to my cry; for I am brought very low: deliver me from my persecutors; for they are stronger than I. Bring my soul out of prison, that I may praise thy name: the righteous shall compass me about; for thou shalt deal bountifully with me" (Psalms 142).

APERÇU

Betrayal and abandonment are common weapons the enemy uses to inflict the pain of rejection.

The Word cast stems from the Hebrew word shalak, meaning to throw, hurl, fling, shed, cast off.

One of the most helpful prayers to pray when someone hurts you is: "Lord I cast all my cares on you because I know that you care for me" (1 Peter 5:7).

The Word sustain stems from the Hebrew word *kuwl*, which means to hold-up, nourish, refresh, support and supply.

Chapter 10

ME, CHOSEN
AND ACCEPTED?

F reedom from rejection is essential to your spiritual
growth. People who suffer with rejection have poor
self-esteem. They often struggle with self-worth. God
has uniquely created each of us with the ability to lay
hold of an identity and attach value to it. Unfortunately,
many times that identity does not come from Christ.
All too often that identity is rooted in rejection. After
an identity is created we can step back, examine it, and
decide if we like it or not. After reading this book, you

may discover that your identity is created in rejection. If so, you can exchange that rejection-based identity for a Christ-based identity. There is life after rejection.

Applying the knowledge of the Word of God in your life can change the way you see yourself. Your feelings and views of self-inadequacy can be renovated with Truth. The critical voice of rejection (internalization) that constantly tears down your value can be disarmed. Benefiting from this book is not as simple as just reading it. You will have to do some work. Don't get disappointed or shrink back from the challenge! You have already begun the work and are well on your way to life after rejection. There are new understandings, exercises, and skills that you will need to lay-hold of, but you are well able. Make a commitment right now to chart a course for freedom. Your feelings of rejection can be replaced by the understanding that you are accepted by the Lord.

NO REJECTION HERE

You are accepted just as you are. God is not rejecting you. These are always comforting Words to those fighting the tormenting feelings of rejection.

"Of a truth I perceive that God is no respecter of persons: But in every nation he that feareth him, and worketh righteousness, is accepted with him (Acts 10:34-35).

It is important for people who suffer with rejection to know that God has not rejected them. Again, they must learn to exchange the feelings of rejection with the knowledge of acceptance. God never intended for us to struggle with feelings of low self-esteem, unworthiness, or rejection. Jesus wants us to understand we have value and worth, not because of who we are in ourselves, but because of who we are in Him. When we fail to accept ourselves in Him, rejection has an open door to our emotions.

Dealing successfully with rejection requires honesty and a willingness to pull out all the roots of our pain, including a poor view of our own self-worth. We can never base our worth as a person on the others' opinions. Nor can we confuse position, titles, works, or status with worth. We are valuable! Jesus thought enough of us to die on the cross for us so we could be free. We are not our own. We belong to Him (1 Corinthians 6:19-20).

Often at church, I see people struggle with rejection when they do not qualify for a particular position of helps in the ministry. In no way does that devaluate them, yet they confuse position with personal value. Throughout the years I have seen people leave the ministry because they did not get a 'coveted position' in the church. This is a grievous thing. Our self-worth or personhood should not be determined by our social position in life. Anytime we base our self-worth on what other people say about us, or our social position in life, we set ourselves up for rejection.

GOD'S OWN POSSESSION

In his first epistle, Peter wrote to a group of believers who were struggling with persecution and deep rejection. Trying to instill a sense of hope in those who would read his letter, Peter heralded their value in the Kingdom of God:

> "You are a chosen race, a royal priesthood, a holy nation, a people for God's own possession, that you may proclaim the excellencies of Him who has called you out of darkness into His marvelous light; for you once were not a people, but now you are the people of God;

you had not received mercy, but now you have received mercy" (1 Peter 2:9-10).

Chosen, royal, holy, and God's very own possession – wow! Peter also lets everyone know that they are special in the Lord's eyes. They are accepted and not rejected. Let's learn to exchange our feelings of rejection for knowledge that the Lord Himself accepts you. Scripture assures us that we are accepted in the beloved" (Ephesians 1:6).

Here's a good place to start. When you begin to feel rejected, verbally pray this prayer: "Thank you, Jesus, that I am accepted and not rejected. You have declared me chosen, royal, holy, and your very own. I am worthy, valuable, useful, and accepted. Right now I exchange these feelings of rejection for the knowledge of the truth; you loved me enough to die for me and I love you enough to live for you."

APERÇU

Getting free from rejection is essential to spiritual growth.

One must learn to exchange the feelings of rejection with the knowledge of acceptance.

When we fail to accept ourselves in Jesus, rejection has an open door to our emotions.

We can never base our worth as a person on others' opinions. Nor can we confuse position, titles, works, or status with worth.

Our self-worth or personhood is never determined by our social position in life. Anytime we base our self-worth on what other people say about us, or our social position in life, we set ourselves up for rejection.

Chapter 11

OH NO!
NOT CORRECTION

If there is anything that people suffering with rejection cannot stand it is correction. Most people who are suffering with rejection would rather take a beating with a stick than be corrected verbally. That's because the rejected take correction as an attack against their self-value. For some twisted reason, correction undermines their sense of self-worth. However, correction is valuable to everybody when administered in the right spirit. People suffering from rejection, then, must learn to recognize the value of correction and even covet it. Without correction we can never learn new skills, or develop emotionally and grow. All of us benefit from correction.

Resistance to correction severely hinders one's ability to mature. God has a cure for this hindrance to our development. Scripture declares, "God hath set some in the church, first apostles, secondarily prophets, thirdly teachers" to help us to grow (1 Corinthians 12:18). These ministries are also referred to as ascension gifts. When Jesus ascended into heaven He sent back gifts to men. Jesus Himself gave these gifts to the Body of Christ. Their ministry calling is to bring every believer into a place of spiritual maturity and activation (Ephesians 4). To mature means to be fully:

- Developed.

- Aged.

- Complete.

Because Jesus gave the Church ascension gift ministers to help believers mature there will always be a demand put on us to grow. Personal growth and maturity is vital for us if we are to complete the Great Commission and fulfill our personal destinies. Correction is necessary for us to mature from babes in Christ to sons of God. There is no escaping the issue.

TRANSITION

True ministers of the Gospel have a father's heart. The father has the best interest of the son in his heart. The assignment of a father is to transition his son into adulthood by preparing him to successfully deal with the responsibilities of life.

In this world we have natural fathers and spiritual fathers. The Apostle Paul said, "For though ye have ten thousand instructors in Christ, yet have ye not many fathers" (1 Corinthians 4:15). The success and well-being of Paul's spiritual sons, like Timothy and Titus, was always in his heart. To be able to help his spiritual sons, however, they had to be willing to submit to any counsel and correction Paul offered. If Paul's spiritual sons were suffering with rejection they would not have been able to fulfill their ministries.

CORRECTION BRINGS ADVANCEMENT

There are several reasons children resist correction, including rebellion, rejection, and self-centeredness. Once a young woman told me that 'she should not have to do anything that she did not want to do.' Her statement revealed the root of my inability to help her mature. Today she still lives in rebellion, away from God. My heart goes out to her because of the mighty call of God on her life that sits awaiting her obedience.

Another one of my spiritual sons told me that he wanted to 'grow at his own pace.' Twelve years later he is still in the same pitiful condition. Without godly counsel and loving correction from those whom God has placed over us we cannot rise to the next level.

TRAINING, INSTRUCTION AND CORRECTION

Through correction, all of us can advance to a level beyond our current abilities. Without learning from our mistakes and failures, on the other hand, there can be no advancement. We simply cannot grow without godly correction. The Word of God speaks much about correction.

"And ye have forgotten the exhortation which speaketh to you as to children, My son, despise not thou the chastening of the Lord, nor faint when thou art rebuked of

> Correction is proof of sonship and the prerequisite for advancement.

him: For whom the Lord loveth he chasteneth, and scourgeth every son whom he receiveth. If ye endure chastening, God dealeth with you as with sons; for what son is he whom the father chasteneth not? But if ye be without chastisement, whereof all are partakers, then are ye bastards, and not sons. Furthermore we have had fathers of our flesh which corrected us, and we gave them reverence: shall we not much rather be in subjection to the Father of spirits, and live? For they verily for a few days chastened us after their own pleasure; but he for our profit, that we might be partakers of his holiness. Now no chastening for the present seemeth to be joyous, but grievous: nevertheless afterward it yieldeth the peaceable fruit of righteousness to them which are exercised thereby" (Hebrews 12: 5-11).

The Word chastening stems from the Greek Word *paidiuo*, meaning to:

- Train.

- Instruct.

- Cause to learn.

- Mold.

- Correct.

People suffering with rejection take everything way too personal. That's why they have a difficult time receiving correction. Correction seems to make them feel less than a person. Rejection tells the person that correction is a direct assault against their sense of value. They see correction as a threat to tear down their self-esteem. However, in reality, we all must learn the value of correction. Correction always prepares us for advancement.

CORRECTION IS PROOF OF SONSHIP

When we are chastened (corrected) by God, either through His Word, His leaders, or through difficult circumstances, it is not a sign of His rejecting us, but His receiving us. God's goal is not to make us miserable, but rather to correct us for our own good. Chastening is proof of sonship. The Word declares,

> "My son, despise not the chastening of the Lord; neither be weary of his correction: For whom the Lord loveth he correcteth; even as a father the son in whom he delighteth" (Proverbs 3:11-12).

If God did not love you, then He would not take the time to correct you. Consider this verse from the Book of Revelation:

"As many as I love, I rebuke (convict) and chasten (correct); be zealous (earnestly pursue) therefore, and repent (change your mind)" (Revelation 3:19).

Unfortunately, Satan has sold the church a counterfeit idea of love. Some wrongly believe this way: "Because God is love I should never be corrected." Satan tells people they should be received and preserved, as is, in a spirit of love. But that kind of love is not genuine. When you love someone, you will not leave him or her in the condition they are in. To allow a person to be ruled by their emotions, or to neglect to challenge a person to move into faith and character development, is not God's love. If a person is not teachable, he will be hindered in his walk with God. If he is not teachable, he will be hindered from growing and maturing in the Lord. Beloved, it is time for all of us to grow up into the fullness of our calling. We cannot remain merely the children of God. We must become the sons of God. So the next time God uses your pastor to correct you, remember this: Correction is proof of sonship and the prerequisite for advancement. It is not an attack against your value as a person.

In the next chapter let's review ways to minister to those with rejection.

APERÇU

People suffering with rejection take correction as an attack against their value.

The rejected must recognize the value of correction and even covet it.

Through correction all of us can advance to a level beyond our current abilities.

Without learning from our mistakes and failures there can be no advancement.

The Word chastening stems from the Greek Word *paidiuo*, meaning to train, instruct, mold, correct, and cause to learn.

When we are chastened (corrected) by God, either through His Word, His leaders, or through difficult circumstances, it is not a sign of His rejecting us. It is a sign of His receiving us.

Correction is proof of sonship and the prerequisite for advancement. It is not an attack against your value as a person.

Chapter 12

MINISTERING TO THOSE WITH REJECTION

Identification is a very important part of ministering to people suffering with rejection. Identification means to put oneself in another's place by understanding and sharing the thoughts, feelings, emotions, and problems of another. Intercession is a form of identification. Identification is closely related to and often mistaken for carnal sympathy. There is a great difference in 'feeling sorry' for someone and identifying with them in an effort to help them.

REACH OUT AND TOUCH ME

Jesus identifies with our suffering. He is our great example of bringing healing to people in need. "For we have not a high priest which cannot be touched with the feeling of our infirmities; but was in all points tempted like as we are, yet without sin" (Hebrews 4:15). We too can be touched with the feelings of others. The Greek expression for "touched with the feeling" is *sumpatheo*, meaning to:

- Have compassion.

- Be affected with the same feeling as another.

- Sympathize with.

- Feel for.

- Identify with.

Also from *sumpatheo* we get our English Word sympathy. Jesus' sympathy is not merely feeling sorry for us. His sympathy is a way of compassionately identifying with our suffering to bring about healing and deliverance.

It is important to those who suffer the pain of rejection to identify with the pain. This may sound trivial, but understanding identification is vital if you are going to be an effective minister to someone suffering with rejection. Identification is the bridge that will connect you to the rejected.

Identifying with the pain of people suffering with rejection will prequalify you as a minister in their eyes. Pain speaks to the rejected, asking them if you can 'feel their pain.' If not, then they will disqualify you to minister to them.

NEGATIVE IDENTIFICATION

There is a potential pitfall for ministers who seek to identify with people suffering with rejection. The rejected may seek out soulish sympathy, consolation and solace from those with common ground. As a minister, you can console someone without ever helping one get free if you pet their flesh and refuse to tell them the truth of God's Word in the matter.

Often those with rejection search for others with the same hurts and wounds – people with common ground – to sympathize with them. Unfortunately, controllers also look for those suffering with rejection. Jezebel easily identifies with one's pain, hurts and wounds. She will use them to control the person, not to set them free. A true minister of the Gospel will never feed into hurts and wounds. The blind can never lead the blind, least they both fall into a ditch (Luke 6:39).

VALUE OF IDENTIFICATON

Still, identification is a valuable tool in the hand of a mature minister. Let me offer you a couple of examples of the value of identification. Many years ago we were replacing some light fixtures in our church building, including two in my office. Of all the lights we replaced in the entire building, the ones in my office would not work correctly. Of course, this annoyed me because I had a mountain of work to do and having poor lighting hindered my productivity. When my wife came into the room, I began to vent my frustration over the lights to

her. Her response? She didn't
want to hear about it. In fact,
she was short with me.

I was taken back by
her lack of concern for my
perilous dilemma. Didn't
she understand I had some

> Rejection tells you
> that your feelings
> are the real you.

important work to do? After all, wasn't I the senior
pastor? Then I found myself getting angry with her.
I began transferring my frustration with the lights
toward her. As I thought about my anger toward
her for not 'understanding my feelings,' I experienced
rejection's operations. Negative feelings plague those
who suffer with rejection. If they don't think that
you are identifying with their pain, then you cannot
minister to them. To those with rejection, the bridge
of communication (identification) is destroyed when
you don't feel the pain.

I learned an interesting lesson from this event.
When my wife did not identify with my aggravation, I
felt she was not connected to me. My negative emotions
were offering a bridge to her that she refused to walk
on. Rejection tells you that your feelings are the real
you. In other words, my feelings of rejection were telling
me this: Because my wife was not identifying with my
aggravation (pain) I was not important. She just blew

me off with a trivial, "I'm too busy to deal with the lights right now." To her it meant that we could handle it later. To me it was an attack against my value.

When you are counseling with a person who suffers with rejection personality malfunctions, make sure you take the time to connect with their pain. Let them spend some time and try their best to explain their feelings. It's important to them for you to make an effort to try to understand them. To keep it in balance, please understand that you are not called to have a co-pity-party with them, but rather to start the healing process off in the spirit of understanding. Rejection is a sneaky thing. People suffering with rejection need to know that you are *trying* to identify with them.

This book is not the forum for an exhaustive work on how a person gets hurt. Suffice it to say the heart of the rejection-based personality malfunction is rooted in some sort of pain. Yes, everybody faces rejection, but the person who has been hurt and wounded will respond to rejection circumstances differently than people who refuse to allow rejection to wound them. If we can remove the pain and exchange feelings for truth, then we can be instruments God uses to help bring healing. Some people are healed instantly from pain while others need more time to work through the past, renew their minds and receive God's healing power. Remember, Jesus is our Great Physician and we can depend on His help. He will never leave us or forsake us.

POINT TOWARD JESUS

I remember a dear friend who was hurled into the chaos of divorce. It was a heart-wrenching experience for him. He tried desperately to save his marriage to no avail. After his divorce was final, he wanted to get on with his life and deal with the issues he now faced as a single believer. So he went to his local church. The leadership was actively promoting a single's ministry and he was excited about the possibilities of a new beginning. However, to his surprise the leader of the group made a disturbing announcement during the first meeting: divorced people could not attend the class.

This rejection of not being included in the group brought his pain back to the surface. It was like having flashbacks. He told me he felt like he was somehow lessened in value because of his divorce. Even though I have been happily married over 29 years and have never been divorced, I identified with his pain and pointed him to Jesus. Then I prayed for him and reassured him that God was still the "author and finisher of his faith"

(Hebrews 12:2). After I prayed for him, I put my arms around him and told him that I loved him, too.

When ministering to people looking to Jesus to get free from hurts, always point them to Jesus. He understands them better than anyone else. Today my friend is happily married to a woman who loves him and they are both serving God. People who are suffering from rejection must lay hold of the unchanging truth that we are loved, accepted, and complete in Christ.

PRAYING FOR THE REJECTED

When I pray for people with inner hurts and wounds, love and compassion overcomes me. Through the anointing, it seems as if I can reach into the depths of their heart, grab hold of that pain and pull it out. Remember this: True compassion for the hurting is always coupled with an urge from the Holy Spirit to help them get free.

It is important to offer more than pity and pray for those who are afflicted with rejection. Remember, the root cause of rejection is some sort of pain. Deliverance is an important key in the process of helping someone who is struggling to break free from a rejection-based personality. Here is a list of some spirits and issues that should be bound in deliverance prayer:

- Self-rejection.

- Abandonment.

- Abuse of all kinds.

- Hurts and wounds.

- False personality.

- Discouragement.

- Anxiety.

- Suspicion.

- Distrust.

- Fear of people's opinion.

- Fear of failure.

- Insecurity.

- Bitterness.

- Shame.

- Guilt.

- Condemnation.

- Unworthiness.

Binding up the emotions and spirits listed above is a good start when you pray for someone suffering from rejection. For an in-depth study of the scriptural foundations for deliverance read my book _Come Out!_[1] I wrote this book as a handbook for the serious deliverance minister. It is a valuable asset to your ministerial library. It has helped hundreds of precious people get free.

APERÇU

Identification means to put oneself in another's place; to understand and share the thoughts, feelings, emotions, and problems of another.

The Greek expression for "touched with the feeling" stems from the *sumpatheo*, meaning to have compassion, be affected with the same feeling as another, sympathize with and feel for (Hebrews 4:15).

Jesus' brand of sympathy does not merely feeling sorry for us. It is a way of compassionately identifying with our suffering to bring about healing and deliverance.

Often people suffering with rejection search for others with the same hurts and wounds (common ground) to sympathize with them.

Rejection tells you that your feelings are the real you.

When you are ministering to people who are getting free from hurts, always point them to Jesus. He understands them better than anyone else (Hebrews 12:2).

People suffering from rejection must lay hold of the unchanging truth that we are loved, accepted, and complete in Christ.

Deliverance is an important key in the process of helping someone who is struggling from the fruit of rejection.

Notes

1 Jonas Clark, *"Come Out,"* (Hallandale, FL. Spirit of Life Publications, 2001)

Chapter 13

THE GATES
OF FORGIVENESS

Many people have been so hurt that they are locked in the pit of rejection and don't know how to escape. I am convinced the hell of rejection has reinforced gates caused by unforgiveness and bitterness. So, how can one escape? The answer is found in our ability to forgive.

Consider Brian, who has a powerful testimony about forgiveness and rejection. Brian lived in a large family with eight brothers and sisters. When Brian was five years old his mother and father separated and left him with his older sisters to raise him.

Since Brian was only five years old, he could not understand why his mother left him. He felt unwanted and unimportant. The truth is, as a single mother she faced a tremendous challenge of raising all the children by herself. She moved to another city to find work and needed time to prepare a place for the children to follow her. It was four long years before Brian saw his mother again. After being reunited with his mother he and his siblings lived together but the experience left a scar.

When Brian was 17 years old his father moved back into the home in an attempt to reunite with his mother. The effort proved fruitless, failing miserably. There were many nights of intensely heated arguments. Chaos ran rampant through the household. The family split. Some of the children sided with the father and others sided with the mother. Brian told me he felt divided and torn because he was standing in the middle. About that time, Brian gave his life to Jesus and was powerfully changed. When he tried to share the Gospel with his family, though, they rejected it and would not receive from him.

That wasn't the extent of his rejection, though. Throughout Brian's teenage years he was overweight. One of his brothers teased him continuously. Brian was so hurt by this chiding that he would cry himself to sleep at night. He felt so alone in that house, even though it was full of people. Brian even thought that his family was not really his family. He wanted to run away from home and look for his real family. After all, how could this be his real family? Brian told me he often dreamed about what his real mother and family would be like if he found them. Even though Brian was born-again he was still suffering from rejection. Without a conscious understanding, he was still harboring unforgiveness and bitterness in his heart toward his mother.

Brian began to attend church on regularly. He liked what he was hearing and felt drawn to other believers. One night at church an Evangelist was speaking about the baptism in the Holy Spirit and the importance of forgiving those who had hurt them. At that moment his heart was compelled to forgive his brother for the constant teasing. When Brian forgave his brother he was instantaneously filled with the Holy Spirit and began to speak in other tongues.

In the days to follow the Holy Spirit continued to deal with Brian's heart about forgiving others. Soon he found himself in a serious argument with his mother. They were yelling and screaming at each another. Then Brian yelled, "Mom, you have never told me that you loved me!" His mother was shocked and stunned. The look on her face was a puzzled amazement. When she heard those words she began to breakdown and cry. Then she said, "Son, I do love you."

Brian went 17 years without a single "I love you" from his mother. When Brian heard those words and saw his mother's tears, he, too, broke down and cried. It was at that moment that he forgave his mother. Through Brian's tears flowed years of pain and hurt. That night rejection was broken and Brian began to grow and mature in the Lord. Someone may have hurt you deeply. Forgiving them, frees you to receive God's forgiveness and restoration in your own life.

THE FORGIVING CHOICE

Like Brian, when you were born again you received the ability to forgive. It became a part of your new nature (2 Corinthians 5:17). Before we describe what forgiveness is, perhaps we should first mention what forgiveness is not. Forgiveness is not denial, tolerating, excusing, condemning, seeking justice, or reconciliation. We should not confuse reconciliation with forgiveness. Reconciliation is when two people who have separated because of a disagreement come back together.

Therefore, it is possible for you to forgive someone without ever gaining reconciliation. It takes two people to reconcile, but only one person to offer forgiveness. So then,

> Forgiveness is not an emotion; it is a decision.

forgiveness is a choice we make by using our wills.

Offering forgiveness has absolutely nothing to do with our feelings. To forgive we simply choose to obey God's Word, "...forgive those who have trespassed against us" (see Matthew 6:12). Forgiveness is not an emotion; it is a decision. God is serious about the issue of forgiveness. He even teaches us that if we do not forgive, then our heavenly Father will not forgive.

"For if ye forgive men their trespasses, your heavenly Father will also forgive you: But if ye forgive not men their trespasses, neither will your Father forgive your trespasses" (Matthew 6:14-15).

We can never allow unforgiveness to lock us up in the past. God sent His only begotten son to die in our place so our sins, faults, and failings could be freely forgiven. As children of God, he expects us to offer the same forgiveness to those who have sinned against us. Jesus said, "For in the same way you judge others, you will be judged, and with the measure you use, it will be measured to you" (Matthew 7:2). You can't store up good feelings toward those that you have forgiven, you can only draw them fresh from God each day. The Holy Spirit is here to help us forgive those who have hurt us. Forgiveness is an essential key that will free you from the pain of rejection.

APERÇU

When you were born again you received the ability to forgive. It became a part of your new nature (2 Corinthians 5:17).

Forgiveness is not denial, tolerating, excusing, condemning, seeking justice, or reconciliation.

Reconciliation is when two people who have separated because of a disagreement come back together.

It is possible for you to forgive someone without ever obtaining reconciliation. It takes two people to reconcile but only one person to offer forgiveness.

Forgiveness is a choice that we make through by using our wills.

Offering forgiveness has absolutely nothing to do with our feelings.

To forgive we simply choose to obey God's Word, " ...forgive those who have trespassed against us" (Matthew 6:12).

Forgiveness is an essential key that will free you from the pain of rejection.

Chapter 14

THE MR. HYDE
SYNDROME

I have passed through many personality malfunctions in my life that were caused by the pain of rejection. This qualifies me, to some degree, to deal with a rejected belief system that stops us from breaking through. In this chapter, I am not going to pull any punches. I am going to get right to the point. The rejected personality is a self-centered, rude, brash, noncivil, Mr. Hyde personality! I know that sounds a bit harsh, but people suffering with rejection know that it is true.

We have a choice. We can study about the emotional scars of yesterday, come to the understanding that we have a problem with rejection, and feel sorry for ourselves – but never change. Or, we can make a decision to overcome the noncivil personality that rejection built. The decision to change is not up to someone else; that decision is up to us. Will it be uncomfortable? Will freedom require us to change? The answer to both questions is, "Yes." But why continue to live the way you are living? Life is more than you can see right now. There is life after rejection.

To change we must break the repetitive patterns that caused us to be the rude and self-centered people that we have become. How is it that a person who suffers from rejection can function at work but becomes a basket case on a personal level? Is it because work is mechanical and relationships are more emotional? Or could it just be caused by a self-centered view of life?

People learn and grow emotionally as a process of interaction with others. However, the rejected will intentionally avoid emotional interactions. I have met many people suffering with rejection problems who had terrible people skills. They have a difficult time communicating and often withdraw themselves into a cocoon.

For example, some isolate themselves in another room when family or others visit. Sometimes this is because they have a fear of communicating inadequately. At other times the isolation is simply the result of the self-centered, noncivil, rejection-based personality. If you don't want to talk about their interest, then they don't want to talk with you at all. To escape the forced interaction with others they say things like, "That's your company." The result is this: they hide in their cave and never grow emotionally.

Yes, I know that people suffering with rejection are touchy, too sensitive, and avoid emotional exercises with others. But I also know they wear their feelings on their sleeves and can be rude at times. Here's why: Since they have spent years guarding the rejection, they are simply lacking in plain, old-fashioned, good manners.

From the standpoint of getting free from rejection, it doesn't matter how much hurt has been inflicted on you. You can't look at that as an excuse. Instead, you have to look toward Jesus, in faith, for the strength and grace to change. To tear down the house rejection built, you are going to have to learn some basic manners and people skills for starters. Begin by being polite to others, even if you don't 'feel' like it. Remembering the golden rule will help you significantly: Do unto others as you would have them do to you. If you are suffering with rejection and have made it up to this point in the book, then please hear me. Now is the time to tear down the Dr.-Jekyll-and-Mr.-Hyde personality and start developing some basic people skills. Being polite, kind, thoughtful, agreeable and friendly may be foreign to you, but if you really want to change, these traits must become part of your new self. You have been uncivil long enough. From this day forward, look at being thoughtful as a social responsibility that you can never afford to overlook again. Don't worry. The Holy Spirit will be right there to help you walk in love with others.

Good manners and basic social skills are valuable in helping to smooth out the rough edges that rejection built. No one is born with communication or people skills. We all have to learn them. So if you see Jekyll and Hyde aspects of your personality, make a decision today to be polite and consider the feelings of others at every turn. You'll be happier that way, too. Come out of the cave of ill manners and force yourself to grow. Everything improves with practice, including civility. Tell the Mr. Hyde personality good-bye. Then live life after rejection. It is an abundant life full of peace and joy with healthy, strong relationships.

ENABLERS

People who have remained emotionally immature could point to a series of enablers throughout their life. I once knew a successful businessman who was extremely self-centered and emotionally immature because of rejection. As we take a look at his life, we will notice a series of enablers who refused to help him grow up.

The first enablers we discover in the man's life are his parents. When he was a child his parents never took the time to discipline and correct his self-centered behavior. His father was seldom home and when he was home he didn't do much to raise the child in the way he should go. Because of parental neglect he was full of emotional maladies when he grew up. His people skills were never developed; he did not respect others, and often suffered from severe bouts of depression.

As a young man he married a woman and they had a child together. But, unlike his parents, his wife refused to allow his self-centered behavior to go unchecked. Whenever she tried to help stabilize him emotionally, however, he took it as an attack against his self-worth and would lash out at her. Because of this cycle, she felt the burden to keep his happiness was her responsibility. Conflict was commonplace in their home. The man became extremely self-centered, controlling, and domineering. Finally, he began to abuse his wife both emotionally and physically. Nine years of turmoil led to a divorce. Most of the conflict in the home was because the man wanted to do whatever he liked without regard to the feelings of others.

The next enablers we find are the man's employees. Many who suffer with rejection are very hard workers. They identify self-worth and value with accomplishments. After the man's divorce he immerged himself in his work and became quite wealthy. His wealth created a prominence in his own eyes. His wealth became his license to continue living in an uncivil and disrespectful manner. People who worked for him tolerated his insolence and abuse because they needed their paycheck. So his employees continued to be enablers. Those who refused to submit to his abuse would either quit or get fired. As the years passed, the man waxed worse and worse.

The final enabler we find in his life was Jezebel. A few years after he divorced his first wife, this man married a woman who was the classic Jezebel gold digger. She married him for his money and allowed him continue in his emotional immaturity. She was good at handling the problems he didn't like to handle. She would even handle his dirty work for him; thus the classic Ahab and Jezebel relationship. The man died shortly after. Jezebel got his money and stole the man's only child's inheritance.

APERÇU

The rejected personality is a self-centered, rude, brash, noncivil, and Mr. Hyde personality!

We can study about the emotional scars of yesterday, come to the understanding that we have a problem with rejection, and feel sorry for ourselves, and still never change.

To change means we must break the repetitive patterns that have caused us to be the rude and self-centered people that we have become.

The rejected are touchy, too sensitive, and avoid emotional exercises with others.

Often people suffering with rejection wear their feelings on their sleeves and can often be extremely rude.

To tear down the house that rejection built, you are going to have to learn some basic manners and people skills. You can start by being polite to others, even if you don't 'feel' like it.

Abiding by the golden rule can significantly help people who have rejection-based, malfunctioning personalities. That rule says, Do unto others as you would have them do unto you."

For a person to remain emotionally immature there must be a series of enablers throughout their life.

Chapter 15

UNRAVELING
REJECTION

P eople suffering from rejection sometimes cast blame, get angry and take the bait of offense. Then they erect defense barriers. Their goal is to protect themselves from what they perceive as the danger of fresh wounds that fortify negative emotions that keep them stranded in emotional turmoil. Others bury themselves in their work. Still others make excuses and turn to alcohol, drugs or food to subdue their emotional pain and mental distress.

In fact, the person's determined unwillingness to face more pain can lead them on the path to addictions. Although the use of prescription drugs, alcohol and illegal substances may provide some short-term relief from pain, these people eventually do severe damage to their lives. Additions of any kind produce destructive patterns and perpetuate – or even worsen – emotional pain. It's a vicious cycle that must be broken by the truth of God's Word and with help from His Spirit.

THE FAMOUS
DISAPPEARING ACT

Some rejection sufferers pull a Houdini act – they completely disappear from the scene. Their mind-set could be expressed this way: "If you want to see me then drop everything you are doing and send out the search party." This disappearing act is an attention-getting display of rejection's work. That sort of manipulation doesn't fly in the real world.

Take aviation, for example. Air traffic controllers can't handle any disappearing acts from pilots. The Federal Aviation Administration, or FAA, requires pilots to close out a flight plan when they arrive at their intended destination. If the pilot doesn't complete this task, the authorities send out a search and rescue party. There are times when pilots forget to cancel their flight plan, later finding themselves in serious trouble with the FAA and facing potentially hefty fines.

> Once a person experiences rejection, he will find rejection even where it does not exist.

People suffering with rejection are also known to disappear from your airspace. When they are internalizing feelings of rejection and flying with the woe-is-me autopilot engaged, you might not see them for weeks. "What's happening?" you ask. They are practicing their famous disappearing act. This is how they deal with their negative emotions and feelings of rejection. They enter a hide-and-seek routine where they expect you to send out the search party and chase them down. The chase seems to give them a sense of value and appreciation. If you don't find them, they don't think you love them or they become indifferent. The rejected will use this chase scene to test your love for them. If you don't respond to them the way they think you should, then they don't think you love them. Once a person experiences rejection, he will find rejection even where it does not exist. I have even seen people who expect to be rejected. Satan will make sure they get what they expect.

Those who internalize their rejected feelings are not interpreting life properly. Stop the malfunction and stay out of the caves of depression and indifference. Don't disappear from the screen of life by running from God and those who love you. When rejection goes off (internalization), run to God and don't isolate yourself.

ALL ABOARD
THE WOE-IS-ME EXPRESS

As a pastor I sometimes feel unfairly treated by those who suffer with rejection. Some make me feel like I am supposed to chase after them and make sure they are alright, their needs are met, and they are happy. I liken it to an emotional roller coaster that people want me to climb aboard. When I don't join in, they get mad at me. It's almost like a form of control. If you miss one opportunity to minister to them, then they show their displeasure and they are long gone. It seems that they put undue pressure and unrealistic expectations on me by trying to transfer their burden onto me rather than onto the Lord. A minister can never board the Woe-Is-Me Express.

PAYBACK IS HELL

It's a proven thing that we will reap what we sow. Scripture says so, and it has been confirmed by thousands. Consider this divorced mother's testimony. For years her children thought she loved God more than she loved them because she would seldom include them in her church activities. In their eyes, God was more important than they were. Remember, Satan takes every opportunity to twist and pervert.

One day when her children were grown and out on their own, she expected them to visit her at her birthday celebration. She was so excited with the opportunity to gather her children together. However, to her surprise, the children never showed up. The next day a phone call came from her oldest son. After asking him why he failed to show for the birthday celebration, the son responded, "We were just paying you back for the times when you went to church instead of being with us." The mother told me, "Payback is hell." Regardless of how people treat us, we must never allow Satan to use the weapon of rejection to separate us from God and our children. We must work for reconciliation of the family unit when hurts and wounds have let the devil in. There is family life after rejection.

LOVE, WHAT'S THAT?

One of rejection's most common traits is the inability to feel loved. Because people suffering rejection pains build internal walls to protect themselves from new hurts, these same walls keep love from getting through. The rejected feel unworthy. They think other people – and God – also view them as unworthy. They believe God's promises are for everyone else but them. They ask themselves, "How could God love me when I don't even love myself?"

When we pray for people suffering from rejection we need to verbally tear down the walls rejection has built and declare them worthy! These walls make people think that they are unworthy, and don't deserve to be loved as they see themselves in the miserable condition that rejection created.

The good news is that God is love and He wants to love you. He wants you to jump into His lap. He wants to wrap His arms around you and give you a big squeeze. He wants you to know that He is there for you. The Word says, "This is what real love is: It is not our love for God; it is God's love for us in sending his Son to take away our sins" (1 John 4:10 NCV). God has already begun displaying His love for us by sending

His Son. He is faithful to finish what He has started. Jesus promised that He would not "leave us nor forsake us" (Hebrews 13:5). When you receive the revelation of God's love for you, you will find life after rejection.

DON'T HELP ME I'M DROWNING

The rejected would rather drown in self-pity than ask for help. Consider Henry, who does every thing he can to gain the acceptance of his co-workers. He is always on time and never leaves work early. If there is anything that needs to be done, Henry is the first to step forward and volunteer.

Henry sounds like the perfect employee, doesn't he? Except Henry has one major problem. Because of rejection, Henry can't say 'no' to anybody. The results are serious because Henry gets piled up and backlogged with so many things to do that he is driven into depression. He works himself to death. Not only that, but Henry would rather drown than ask for help. Why? Because those with rejection think asking for help is a sign of weakness. Henry looks for acceptance in what he does. This makes him a performance-orientated worker. After a few months at Henry's new job, he enters the 'never-say-no' and 'never-ask-for-help' routine, finding himself unable to perform. Since he is performance-orientated and will not ask for help he continually sets himself up to fail. As a result, Henry's co-workers and supervisors look on him as unfaithful, unable to keep his word, and unable to perform his duties. Soon people avoid associating with him, his employer dismisses him and rejection completes its assignment. It becomes a endless cycle.

REJECTION FLASHBACKS

Sometimes things happen that trigger a memory of a painful event from our past. One young woman told me every time she heard a particular song on the radio it brought back memories of her boyfriend's rejection. Every time she heard the song, she had to deal with the pain again. I call this a rejection flashback.

The devil doesn't do anything new. What worked on you before he will try again. If you get hit by a rejection flashback, take it captive with the Word of God. Rejection flashbacks are trigger mechanisms of pain. Arrest and exchange those feelings with the Word of God. Scripture says,

"For though we walk in the flesh, we do not war
after the flesh: For the weapons of our warfare
are not carnal, but mighty through God to
the pulling down of strongholds. Casting
down imaginations, and every high thing that
exalteth itself against the knowledge of God,
and bringing into captivity every thought to the
obedience of Christ" (2 Corinthians 10: 3-5).

OTHER REJECTION EXAMPLES

Dealing with feelings of rejection is not anything new.
We can and will overcome! Others have...

Jesus was rejected, despised, unappreciated,
acquainted with sorrows and grief (Isaiah
53:3, John 1:11, Matthew 8:34, 27:46). He is
King of Kings and Lord of Lords.

Noah was rejected for 120 years. Can you
imagine building a boat when it had never
rained? Noah turned away from the mockery
of people, obeyed God and kept on building
(Genesis 7).

Job's wife rejected him when she said, "Curse God and die" (Job 2:9). His friends also rejected him, but he forgave and God blessed him mightily (Job 19:19).

Joseph was rejected by his brothers and sold into slavery (Genesis 37:4). Even in the pit of abandonment, he held fast to his dream. Joseph became second only to Pharaoh in Egypt. John the Baptist suffered from ministerial rejection by the religious leaders of Israel, but his voice made a way for Christ even in the wilderness (Matthew 11:18).

Elijah felt the pains of rejection when he declared, "I'm the only one left" (1 Kings 19:14). Soon a chariot of fire escorted him to heaven.

UNDOING REJECTION

It is possible to undo what rejection has done by taking responsibility for your own actions and acknowledging your feelings. Share what is bothering you with Jesus and your pastor. Rejection's house is built by:

- Habit.

- Learned behaviors.

- Thought processes.

- Assumptions.

- Negative internalized feelings.

If we have a rejection-based personality, the way we respond to our emotions must change. We must learn to put others first, be generous and challenge those feelings of rejection. We don't want to merely relieve the symptoms of rejection. We want to change our core beliefs with the Word of God. We must receive correction, set goals for improving our skills, and develop our ability to express ourselves. By following these examples one can learn to enjoy life. So in a nutshell the rejected must:

- Identify the source of rejection and the accompanying feelings.

- Seek deliverance from hurts, wounds, and pain (Luke 4:18).

- Reaffirm your accepted position in Christ (Ephesians 2:6).

- Cast all your cares on Jesus and tell Him exactly what you are feeling (1 Peter 5:7).

- Renew (renovate) your mind with truth (Romans 12:2).

- Forgive those who have hurt you (Matthew 6:12-15).

- Tear down the personality that rejection built.

- Learn new communication and people skills.

- Accept correction as a valuable benefit (Hebrews 12).

- Refuse to take things personally by internalizing negative feelings.

- Follow David's example by turning away, stating your cause and prophesying your future.

APERÇU

Although the use of prescription drugs, alcohol and illegal substances may provide some short-term relief from pain, these people eventually do severe damage to their lives.

People suffering from rejection are notorious for disappearing acts.

A minister can never board the Woe-Is-Me Express.

One of the most common traits of rejection is the inability to feel loved.

The rejected feel unworthy and think God and others also view them as unworthy.

The rejected believe God's promises are for everyone but them.

The rejected are performance-orientated workers who look for acceptance in what they do.

Rejection flashbacks are trigger mechanisms of pain.

REFERENCE DEFINITIONS

The following is a short list of definitions for common words and phrases used in this book.

ADULLAM, CAVE OF
Cave of justice.

ARMOR BEARER
From the Hebrew word *nasa*, meaning to lift, support, sustain, aid, and assist.

CAST
From the Hebrew word *shalak* meaning to throw, hurl, fling, shed, cast off.

CHASTENING
From the Greek word *paidiuo* meaning to train, instruct, cause to learn, mold, and correct.

DECEIVE
From the Greek word *paralogizomai*, meaning to reckon wrong, cheat yourself, false reasoning, delude, circumvent.

DECEPTION
A condition caused by refusing to walk out (obey) the Word of God.

DESPISE
From the Hebrew word *bazah*, meaning to view as worthless.

FORGIVENESS
A choice we make by using our wills.

FORSAKEN
From the Hebrew word *azab*, meaning to depart, leave, desert, forsake, neglect, and abandon.

IDENTIFICATION
To put oneself in another's place, to understand and share the thoughts, feelings, emotions, and problems of another.

ITERNALIZE
To take rejection personally by making it your own.

JEALOUS
Resentfully suspicious, envious.

TAKE
From the Hebrew word *laqach*, meaning to lay-hold of, seize, carry away, win to himself, capture, remove.

MATURE
Fully developed, aged, completed.

RECONCILIATION
When two people who have separated because of a disagreement come back together.

REJECTION
The feeling of not being liked, accepted, loved, valued, or received. It is the state of feeling unwanted, unaccepted, or unappreciated.

SUSTAIN
From the Hebrew word *kuwl*, meaning to hold-up, nourish, refresh, support and supply.

SNARE
From the Hebrew word *mowqesh*, meaning to bait, lure, or trap.

SOUL
The mind, will, intellect, reasoning, imaginations and emotions.

SYMPATHY
The Greek expression for "touched with the feeling" is *sumpatheo*, meaning to have compassion, to be affected with the same feeling as another, to sympathize with, feel for, and identify with. This is the Greek word from which we get our English word "sympathy."

TRANSFORMED
The Greek Word *metamorphoo*, meaning to be changed into another form. This teaches us the Word of God, when used to renovate our minds, will gradually morph us into a person with a Christ-like personality.

SCRIPTURE REFERENCES

"For ye are dead, and your life is hid with Christ in God. When Christ, who is our life, shall appear, then shall ye also appear with him in glory. Mortify therefore your members which are on the earth; fornication, uncleanness, inordinate affection, evil concupiscence, and covetousness, which is idolatry: For which things' sake the wrath of God cometh on the children of disobedience: In which ye also walked some time, when ye lived in them. But now ye also put off all these; anger, wrath, malice, blasphemy, filthy communication out of your mouth. Lie not one to another, seeing that ye have put off the old man with his deeds; And have put on the new man, which is renewed in knowledge after the image of him that created him: Where there is neither Greek nor Jew, circumcision nor uncircumcision, Barbarian, Scythian, bond nor free: but Christ is all, and in all. Put on therefore, as the elect of God, holy and beloved, bowels of mercies, kindness, humbleness of mind, meekness, longsuffering; forbearing one another, and forgiving one another, if any man have a quarrel against any: even as Christ forgave you, so also do ye. And above all these things put on charity, which is the bond of perfectness. And let the peace of

God rule in your hearts, to which also ye are called in one body; and be ye thankful" (Colossians 3:3-15). "Wherefore, my beloved, as ye have always obeyed, not as in my presence only, but now much more in my absence, work out your own salvation with fear and trembling" (Philippians 2:12).

"Not as though I had already attained, either were already perfect: but I follow after, if that I may apprehend that for which also I am apprehended of Christ Jesus" (Philippians 3:12).

"Wherefore laying aside all malice, and all guile, and hypocrisies, and envies, and all evil speakings, As newborn babes, desire the sincere milk of the Word, that ye may grow thereby: If so be ye have tasted that the Lord is gracious" (1 Peter 2:1-3).

"Let the Word of Christ dwell in you richly in all wisdom; teaching and admonishing one another in psalms and hymns and spiritual songs, singing with grace in your hearts to the Lord" (Colossians 3:16).

"For the Word of God is quick, and powerful, and sharper than any two-edged sword, piercing even to the dividing asunder of soul and spirit, and of the joints and marrow, and is a discerner of the thoughts and intents of the heart" (Hebrews 4:12).

"I die daily" (1 Corinthians 15:31).

"For which cause we faint not; but though our outward man perish, yet the inward man is renewed day by day" (2 Corinthians 4:16).

"Casting down imaginations, and every high thing that exalteth itself against the knowledge of God, and bringing into captivity every thought to the obedience of Christ" (2 Corinthians 10:5).

"But we all, with open face beholding as in a glass the glory of the Lord, are changed into the same image from glory to glory, even as by the Spirit of the Lord" (2 Corinthians 3:18).

"Wherefore he is able also to save them to the uttermost that come unto God by him, seeing he ever liveth to make intercession for them" (Hebrews 7:25).

"Being confident of this very thing, that he which hath begun a good work in you will perform it until the day of Jesus Christ…" (Philippians 1:6)

"But he answered and said, every plant, which my heavenly Father hath not planted, shall be rooted up" (Matthew 15:13).

"For a good tree bringeth not forth corrupt fruit; neither doth a corrupt tree bring forth good fruit. For every tree is known by his own fruit. For of thorns men do not gather figs, nor of a bramble bush gather they grapes. A good man out of the good treasure of his heart bringeth forth that which is good; and an evil man out of the evil treasure of his heart bringeth forth that which is evil: for of the abundance of the heart his mouth speaketh" (Luke 6:43-45).

"And why call ye me, Lord, Lord, and do not the things which I say? Whosoever cometh to me, and heareth my sayings, and doeth them, I will show you to whom he is like: He is like a man which built an house, and digged deep, and laid the foundation on a rock: and when the flood arose, the stream beat vehemently upon that house, and could not shake it: for it was founded upon a rock. But he that heareth, and doeth not, is like a man that without a foundation built an house upon the earth; against which the stream did beat vehemently, and immediately it fell; and the ruin of that house was great" (Luke 6:46-49).

"And he said to them all, If any man will come after me, let him deny himself, and take up his cross daily, and follow me. For whosoever will save his life shall lose it: but whosoever will lose his life for my sake, the same shall save it" (Luke 9:23-24).

"A new heart also will I give you, and a new spirit will I put within you: and I will take away the stony heart out of your flesh, and I will give you an heart of flesh. And I will put my spirit within you, and cause you to walk in my statutes, and ye shall keep my judgments, and do them" (Ezekiel 36:26-27).

"The spirit of the Lord GOD is upon me; because the LORD hath anointed me to preach good tidings unto the meek; he hath sent me to bind up the brokenhearted, to proclaim liberty to the captives, and the opening of the prison to them that are bound; To proclaim the acceptable year of the LORD, and the day of vengeance of our God; to comfort all that mourn; To appoint unto them that mourn in Zion, to give unto them beauty for ashes, the oil of joy for mourning, the garment of praise for the spirit of heaviness; that they might be called trees of righteousness, the planting of the LORD, that he might be glorified" (Isaiah 61:1-3).

"Every branch in me that beareth not fruit he taketh away: and every branch that beareth fruit, he purgeth it, that it may bring forth more fruit" (John 15:2).

"But speaking the truth in love, may grow up into him in all things, which is the head, even Christ..." (Ephesians 4:15)

Invitation to Destiny

Are you hungry for more of God? In addition to preaching the Gospel around the world, we also pastor a powerful, Spirit-filled church in South Florida. The Spirit of God told us to build a church from which to send forth believers that could reach their cities and impact the nations for Jesus Christ.

Have you been searching for God only to find religion? Spirit of Life Ministries (SOLM) is a multicultural church where all races gather together in unity and cares for the needs of the whole family. Is something missing from your life? SOLM is a church where you can receive what you need from the Lord. We believe in divine healing, manifesting the gifts of the Spirit, prayer results, miracles, prosperity, finding purpose and making a difference. With God all things are possible.

Are you looking for a place to grow? SOLM is a new apostolic church with all five-fold ministry gifts operating. We have a prophetic call and mandate to equip, activate and release every believer into the work of the ministry according to Ephesians 4:11-12. We invite you to come and connect with your destiny and receive confirmation, impartation and activation for your life.

Come adventure with us,
Jonas and Rhonda Clark

Spirit of Life Ministries World Headquarters
27 West Hallandale Beach Blvd. • Hallandale Beach, Fla. 33009
800.943.6490 • www.JonasClark.com

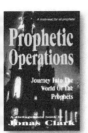
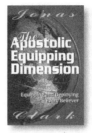

Want to read more about enjoying
life after rejection?

Find answers in THE VOICE® magazine.

Sign up to receive a
FREE Issue of THE VOICE® magazine
at www.thevoicemagazine.com

Seducing Goddess of War

Don't let this spirit control your life!

JONAS CLARK

ISBN 1-886885-04-4

The Jezebel spirit wants to control your life – and then she wants to destroy it. Jezebel is a warring, contending spirit that uses flattery and manipulation to create soul ties that she uses to control her victims... and she's targeting you. Find out how to recognize this spirit's wicked operations, which include false prophecy, fear tactics, seduction and many other wiles. This book will expose this controlling spirit for what it is with explicit details, intriguing personal testimonies and letters from believers who have battled this foe. Don't tolerate Jezebel... get equipped and gain victory over this spirit today!

Revelation about the Jezebel spirit is one thing - practical ways to overcome this evil spirit is another. Find out what REALLY WORKS to stop the Jezebel spirit.

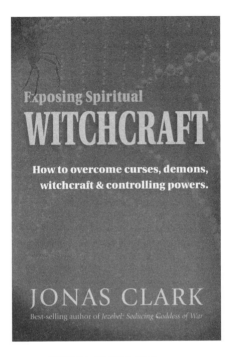

ISBN 1-886885-00-1

Spiritual witchcraft is probably attacking you – whether or not you know it. Every believer needs to learn how to recognize the weapons of witchcraft and be equipped with practical strategies to overcome it.

Spiritual witchcraft is the power of Satan. Its weapons are emotional manipulation, spiritual and religious control, isolation, soul ties, fear, confusion, loss of personal identity, sickness, depression and prophetic divination. Those caught in the snare of this spirit struggle throughout their Christian lives to remain stable. In order to successfully battle spiritual witchcraft you must thoroughly understand your rights as children of God because this demonic force craves to enslave those who are ignorant to the truth.

"I fought this spirit from April to November and won. So can you!"
– Author, Jonas Clark

To order, log on to www.JonasClark.com
or call 800.943.6490.

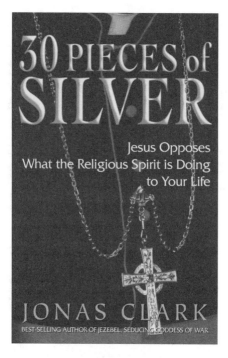

ISBN 1-886885-18-4

When Judas betrayed Jesus he was paid thirty pieces of silver. When he tried to return the money the chief priests said, "This money was paid to have a man killed. We can't put it in the temple treasury." They could pay, we learn, for Jesus' murder with the silver, but they couldn't put it back in the church's bank account. That's the murderous spirit of religion that is still lurking about actively seeking to destroy His Church and your life. The religious spirit did not disappear after the resurrection of Jesus. Perhaps you have heard the voice of a religious spirit before saying things like:

"We don't let that kind come into our church."
"And you call yourself a Christian."
"You are being judgmental."
"Lord, bless this meal."

Religion is your enemy, not your friend.

To order, log on to www.JonasClark.com
or call 800.943.6490.

Dominion • Authority • Purpose

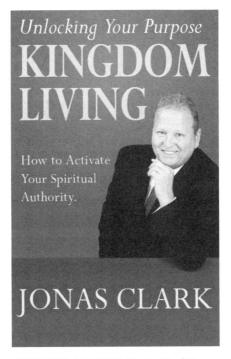

ISBN 978-1-886885-21-9 - HardCover

Are you experiencing Kingdom Living?

Jonas' latest work shows you how to activate your kingship and live the life of purpose, authority and dominion that belongs you in Christ.

Kingdom Living offers practical insights into what Jesus meant when He said, "It is the Father's good pleasure to give unto you the Kingdom." This book unlocks mysteries of the Kingdom for your life. When you read Kingdom Living you will discover how to tap into the power of the Kingdom of God in you and how to pray the way Jesus prayed.

Kingdom Living equips you with action steps designed to help you experience what the Bible says about restoration, dominion, spiritual authority -- and your role in the Kingdom of God.

Free Newsletter

Receive bi-weekly FREE articles
from Jonas Clark to equip you for your destiny.
Read present truth on topics such
as apostolic ministry, spritual warfare,
deliverance, prophetic ministry, Kingdom
living and more.

Sign up today @
www.JonasClark.com